THE

WILD SILKS OF INDIA

THE

WILD SILKS OF INDIA PRINCIPALLY TUSSER

THOMAS WARDLE

GYAN

Published by

Gyan Publishing House
5, Ansari Road
Daryaganj, New Delhi-110002
Phone: 011-47034999, 9811692060
E-mail: books@gyanbooks.com

Distribution Network
gyanbooks.com
India, USA, Canada, UK, Australia

ISBN: 978-93-6433-678-9 (PB)

First Published, 1880

2nd Impression 2024

Printed at: Gyan Press, Delhi.

THE WILD SILKS OF INDIA
Author: THOMAS WARDLE

THE

WILD SILKS OF INDIA,

PRINCIPALLY TUSSER,

BY

THOMAS WARDLE, F.C.S., F.G.S., &c.

Reprinted from the "Journal of the Society of Arts," May 9, 1879.

LONDON:
PRINTED BY GEORGE EDWARD EYRE AND WILLIAM SPOTTISWOODE,
PRINTERS TO THE QUEEN'S MOST EXCELLENT MAJESTY.
FOR HER MAJESTY'S STATIONERY OFFICE.

1880.

ON

THE WILD SILKS OF INDIA,

PRINCIPALLY TUSSER.

INTRODUCTION.

This interesting and important subject has received so much learned attention during the last fifty years, from both entomologists and sericulturalists, that it is impossible now to treat of it in a lecture without saying much that is not absolutely new.

Whilst, therefore, abstract research may have but a narrow field left, I hope that what I have to say may be useful in stimulating a greater utilisation of these products, which are as beautiful as they are curious, and in calling the attention of manufacturers, printers, dyers, and users to some most important improvements and developments in each of their several departments, the result of a lengthened study of the exact nature of the fibres, and of new and improved modes of manufacturing and decorating them.

Amongst the many names of persons in various countries interested in the cultivation of wild silkworms, the utilisation of their products, and in the entomology of the subject, I venture to give the following list, which will be found interesting by many, and will serve to show more forcibly to what a large extent this important subject has been made a matter for study and investigation :—

English.

Dr. Roxburgh, Captain Hutton, Mr. Hugon, Dr. Birdwood, Mr. F. Moore, Mr. P. H. Gosse, Captain Mitchell, Mr. Butler, Major Coussmaker, Lady D. Neville, Lady Gilbert, Mr. Calvert, Mr. Geoghegan, Dr. Alex. Wallace, Dr. Mackenzie, and others.

Continental.

M. Guérin Méneville, M. Personnat, M. Robert, M. Camille Mayne, M. W. Reed, M. Braine, M. Maurice Girard, M. Wailly, Wilhelm Carl Berg, M. Costa, M. Matthieu Bonagous, Mich. Judizky, Roo Van Westmas, N. H. de Graaf, Dr. Chavannes, and many others. My friend, M. Rondot, member of the Chamber of Commerce, Lyons, and President of the Jury, Class 34, Silks, at the Paris Exhibition last year, author of several important works on silk and Eastern dyes, is at the present time giving much economic attention to this question, for the purpose of considering supply for the increasing demand of the French silk trade in wild silks.

Amongst those who have interested themselves especially in the utilisation of these wild silks must be mentioned Dr. Birdwood, who was one of the first, if not the first, to call public attention to the importance of Tusser silk, in a lengthy report to Government in 1858, which I regret I have not time to read.

Lady Dorothy Neville is well known by her efforts in trying to acclimatise the *ailanthus* worm, and in utilising its silk during a long series of observations of a practical nature.

Mr. Geoghegan is the author and compiler of a valuable report to the Government of India on the silk industry of India, which is indispensable to a study of the subject.

Major Coussmaker is pursuing with a praiseworthy determination, at Poonah, his culture of Tusser silkworms, with a view of making Tusser silk as systematic an industry as that produced by *Bombyx mori* and the other mulberry silks.

Besides many others, the enthusiastic labours of the French, aided by their Société d'Acclimatation, set us a great example. They have succeeded in domesticating, if not in almost naturalising, several eastern species of wild silk producers, and in obtaining from them silk of industrial value.

Y 1466. 500.—10/80. I. 1758. A 2

Classification.

The silk-producing *Lepidopterous* insects are of many species, possessing, as is here shown, very marked structural differences, whilst the variety and quiet beauty of their colours and, with the exception of the mulberry feeders, their large size, contribute greatly to the charm of studying this branch of natural history, and they make a collection, apart from their great usefulness, worthy of being placed in the first rank.

They belong, as I have stated, to the order *Lepidoptera,* and are all members of but two families, *Bombycidæ* and *Saturniidæ.*

All the *Saturniidæ* are silk spinners, but not all the *Bombycidæ.*

The British Museum catalogue contains the names of 294 species of *Saturniidæ.* Mr. Butler, of the British Museum, informs me there have been 100 more species added since the publication of the catalogue.

The following table shows the position of these two families in the great system of classification of the animal kingdom, and the known number of Indian genera in each :—

DIVISION III.

Articulata.

SUB-DIVISION II.

Anthropoda (or true articulata).

CLASS VIII.

Insecta.

SUB-CLASS III.

Metabola.

ORDER X.

Lepidoptera.

SUB-ORDER I.

Heterocera (Moths—8 groups or tribes).

GROUP.

Bombycina.

FAMILY 10.

Genera.—Bombycidæ.

Bombyx,	Ocinara,
Theophila,	Trilocha.

FAMILY 8.

Genera.—Saturniidæ.

Attacus,	Caligula,
Antheræa,	Neoris,
Actias,	Saturnia,
Salassa,	Loepa,
Rinaca,	Cricula.
Rhodia,	

Mr. Frederic Moore, curator of the India Museum, the acknowledged authority on Indian wild silk moths, has kindly furnished me with a list of all the silk-producing *Lepidoptera* of India known at the present time.

The new India Museum contains a collection of the principal wild silk moths, with specimens of the cocoons and the silk of their larvæ, arranged by Mr. Moore, a description of which will be found in the second volume of the catalogue on Indian *Levidoptera,* published in 1858–9.

To illustrate my lecture, I have here to-night a very interesting collection of the moths of the greatest industrial importance, as well as the cocoons of their larvæ, and examples of their silk in most, if not all, the various stages of industrial development.

The following is Mr. Moore's list of all the known species of silk producers in India. It is the most valuable list yet published, and shows how rich India is in silk-producing insects :—

Mulberry-feeding Silkworms—Domesticated.

Bombyx mori (Linnæus).—The common silkworm, domesticated in China, Japan, Bokhara, Afghanistan, Cashmere, Persia, S. Russia, Turkey, Egypt and Algeria, Italy, France, and Spain, in all which countries it produces but one crop annually, spinning the largest cocoon and the best silk, of a golden yellow or white.

Bombyx textor (Hutton).—The *Boro poolloo* of Bengal, domesticated in S. China and Bengal; an annual only, producing a white (sometimes yellow) cocoon, of a different texture and more flossy than *B. mori*.

Bombyx sinensis (Hutton).—The *Sina, Cheena,* or small Chinese monthly worm of Bengal, partially domesticated in Bengal, where it was introduced from China; produces several broods in the year; cocoon white and yellow.

Bombyx crœsi (The *Nistry* or *Madrassee* of Bengal, introduced from China; domesticated in Bengal; yielding seven or eight broods of golden yellow cocoons in the year, of larger size than *B. sinensis*.

Bombyx fortunatus (Hutton).—The *Dasee* of Bengal yields several broods annually, spinning the smallest cocoon, of a golden yellow colour.

Bombyx arracanensis (Hutton).—The Burmese silkworm, domesticated in Arracan, said to have been introduced from China through Burmah; yields several broods annually; cocoons larger than the Bengal monthly species.

Mulberry-feeding Silkworms—Wild.

Theophila Huttoni (Westwood).—The wild silkworm of the N. W. Himalayas. A wild species, the worms being found abundantly feeding on the indigenous mulberry in the mountain forests of the N. W. Himalayas.

Theophila sherwilli (Moore).—The wild silkworm of the S. E. Himalayas.

Theophila Bengalensis (Hutton).—The wild silkworm of Lower Bengal. Discovered in the neighbourhood of Calcutta feeding on *Artocarpus lacoocha*. Found also at Ranchee in Chota Nagpore.

Theophila religiosæ (Helfer).—The *Joree* of Assam and *Deo-mooga* of Cachar. Feeds on the bur tree (*Ficus indica*) and the pipul (*F. religiosæ*).

Theophila mandarina (Moore).—The wild silkworm of Chekiang, N. China. Worms stated to feed on wild mulberry trees, spinning a white cocoon.

Ocinara lactea (Hutton).—Mussooree, N. W. Himalaya. Feeds on *Ficus venosa*, spinning a small yellow cocoon, yielding several broods during the summer.

Ocinara Moorei (Hutton).—Mussooree, N. W. Himalaya. Also feeds on *Ficus venosa*, as well as on the wild fig, spinning a small white cocoon. It is a multivoltine.

Ocinara diaphana (Moore).—Khasia hills.

Trilocha varians (Walker).—N. and S. India.

Atlas and Eria Group.

Attacus atlas (Linnæus).—China, Burmah, India, Ceylon, Java. This appears to be almost omnivorous, feeding in different districts upon the shrubs and trees peculiar to it. At Mussooree it is found upon *Bradleia ovata, Falconeria insignis*, and several other trees; at Almorah the yellow flowering barberry is said to be its favourite food. In Cachar it feeds on various other trees. Cocoon well stored with a fine silk.

Attacus silhetica (Helfer).—Silhet.

Attacus Edwardsia (White).—Sikkim, Cherra, and Khasia hills.

Attacus cynthia (Drury).—China. Domesticated in the provinces of Shantung and Honan. Feeds on the varnish tree (*Ailanthus glandulosa*).

Attacus Ricini (Jones).—The *Eria* of Assam, and *Arindi* of Dinajpore. Domesticated in the Northern parts of Bengal (Bogra, Rungpore, and Dinajpore), in Assam and Cachar, feeding on the castor-oil plant (*Ricinus communis*), yielding seven or more crops annually. Cocoons somewhat loose and flossy, orange red, sometimes white. The so-called "Ailanthus silkworm" of Europe—the result of a fertile hybrid between the Chinese and the Bengal species—was produced some years ago in France, by Monsieur Guérin-Méneville, and subsequently reared, from whence it was introduced into various parts of the world.

Attacus Canningi (Hutton).—N. W. Himalayas. Common in a wild state, feeding on the leaves of *Coriaria nipalensis* and *Xanthophyllum hostile*. Cocoons hard and compactly woven, rusty orange or grey. An annual.

Attacus lunula (Walker).—Silhet.

Attacus obscurus (Butler).—Cachar. Not very common. Stated to feed on a plant called *Lood*.

Attacus Guerini (Moore).—Eastern Bengal.

Actias Group.

Actias Selene (McLeay).—Mussooree, Sikkim, and Khasia hills; Madras. The worms feed upon *Andromeda ovalifolia*, *Coriaria nipalensis*, wild cherry, and walnut, at Mussooree, and on *Odina wodier* in Madras.

Actias Sinensis (Walker).—N. China.

Actias Leto (Doubleday).—Sikkim and Khasia hills.

Actias Mœnas (Doubleday).—Sikkim and Khasia hills.

Actias ignescens (Moore).—Andaman Isles.

Tusser and Moonga Group.

Antheræa mylitta (Drury); *Antheræa paphia* of authors; the *Tusser*, *Tussar*, or *Tussah* silkworm.—These well-known and valuable insects (of various undetermined species) are widely distributed over India, from east to west and north to south, on the coast, and in the Central Provinces. They feed in a wild state upon the ber (*Zizyphus jujuba*), the asun (*Terminalia alata*), the seemul (*Bombax heptaphyllum*), &c.

Antheræa mezankooria (Moore); the *Mezankoorie* silkworm of the Assamese.—The worms which produce the mezankoorie silk are stated to feed on the addakoory (? *Tetranthera sp.*), which is abundant in Upper and Lower Assam. The silk is nearly white, its value being fifty per cent. above that of the moonga.

Antheræa nebulosa (Hutton).—This is the *Tusser* of the Sonthal jungles of Colong. It is also found in Singbhoom, Chota Nagpore.

Antheræa Perrotteti (Guér. Mén.).—Described as being found in the districts of Pondicherry, feeding upon a species of *Zizyphus*, the jambool (*Syzygium jambolanum*), &c. Stated to produce four broods in a year.

Antheræa Andamana (Moore).—An allied species to the tusser. Inhabits the S. Andamans.

Antheræa Frithi (Moore).—Sikkim, Himalayas. A common species, inhabiting the hot sub-tropical valleys below 2,000 ft. Known only as a wild species. The cocoon is stated to be similar to that of the tusser in form, but of finer silk.

Antheræa Helferi (Moore).—Sikkim, Himalayas. This is a common species found in the hot valleys of Sikkim.

Antheræa Assama (Helfer).—The *Moonga* or *Mooga* of the Assamese. The moonga silkworm feeds upon the trees known in Assam as the champa (*Michelia sp.*), the soom, kontoolva, digluttee (*Tetranthera diglottica*), the pattee shoonda (*Laurus obtusifolia*), and the Sonhalloo (*Tet. macrophylla*). It is extensively cultivated by the natives, and can be reared in houses, but is fed and thrives best in the open air and upon the trees. The silk forms an article of export from Assam, and leaves the country generally in the shape of thread.

Antheræa Roylei (Moore).—The oak-feeding silkworm of the N. W. Himalayas. A common species, feeding on the hill oak (*Quercus incana*) of the N. W. Himalayas (Simla, Masuri, Almora). The cocoon is large and very tough, the silk being pronounced as promising, and worth cultivating. They can be reared easily in the house.

Miscellaneous Group.

Salassa Lola (Westwood).—Sikkim, Himalayas.

Rinaca Zuleika (Hope).—Sikkim.

Rhodia Newara (Moore).—Nepal (Kathmandoo). Worms feed upon a species of weeping willow. Spins a brilliant green cocoon, pendant from the twigs.

Caligula Thibeta (Westwood).—Mussooree, N. W. Himalayas, 7,000 ft. Common, the worms feeding on *Andromeda ovalifolia*, wild pear, and the cultivated quince, forming a light, open, net-like cocoon.

Caligula Simla (Westwood).—Simla, N. W. Himalayas, 5,000 ft. Feeds on the walnut, *Salix babylonica*, wild pear, &c.; forms an open, net-like cocoon.

Caligula Cachara (Moore).—Cachar.

Neoris Huttoni (Moore).—Mussooree, N. W. Himalaya, 6,500 feet. The worms appear in April, feeding upon a species of wild pear tree; spins a thin silken cocoon.

Neoris Shadulla (Moore).—Yarkund.

Neoris Stoliczkana (Felder).—Ladak.

Saturnia Cidosa (Moore).—Hot valleys of the Sikkim, Himalayas.

Saturnia Grotei (Moore).—Sikkim, Himalayas.

Saturnia Lindia (Moore).—Sikkim, Himalayas.

Saturnia Anna (Moore).—Sikkim, Himalayas.

Loepa katinka (Westwood).—Sikkim, 5,000 to 7,000 feet. Assam.

Loepa sikkima (Moore).—Hot valleys of Sikkim.

Loepa sivalica (Hutton).—Mussooree, 5,000 feet. Spins a long cocoon, pointed at each end, and of a dark greenish-grey colour.

Loepa miranda (Moore).—Sikkim, Himalayas.

Cricula trifenestrata (Helfer); the *Haumpottonee* of the Assamese.—Noted as being very common in Assam, the worms feeding on the soom tree, forming an open net-like cocoon of a beautiful yellow colour and of a rich lustre, the silk being spun in the same manner as the Eria cocoon. Occurs also in Moulmein, where the worms are stated to feed upon the cashew-nut tree (*Anacardium orientale*).

Cricula drepanoides (Moore).—Sikkim.

To this number may be added a few others which, although not of India, are well worth the attention of the Government of India for the purpose of acclimatisation there.

Antheræa Pernyi (Guér. Mén.).—The oak-feeding silkworm of Mantchouria, N. China. This is described as having been long known to the Mantchour Tartars, very large quantities of the silk being used among the Chinese. The worms feed on various species of oak (*Quercus mongolica*), &c., the cocoon differing from the tusser in form and texture. The silk is represented as strong, but with little lustre. Two crops of silk are produced in the year—a spring and autumn crop.

Antheræa Confuci (Moore).—A species allied to *A. pernyi,* inhabiting the hills in the neighbourhood of Shanghai, N. China.

Antheræa Yama-mai (Guérin Méneville).—The *Yama-mai* silkworm of Japan.

An oak-feeding species, forming a cocoon of a pale yellowish-green colour. This worm feeds on the oak, and produces excellent silk of considerable commercial value in Japan. I should strongly recommend its introduction into India. It has been acclimatised in Europe, and crossed with *Bombyx Attacus Pernyi*, is successfully reared in France, the eggs hatching at almost freezing point. The silk is much cultivated and used in Japan. Its fibre is oval, and 950th of an inch thick.

Saturnia pyretorum, from South China.—The worm feeds upon the *Liquidamber formosanu* in Canton, Amoy, where the silk is stated to be woven into a coarse fabric.

Neoris shadulla (Moore).—Yarkund.

Theophila mandarina (Moore).—N. China.

History of Silk.

A few words on the silk of commerce and its history may form a fit preface in introducing to your notice those wild silks which it is my object to describe to-night.

The name silk is derived from the name of the people of Eastern Asia whom the ancient Greeks called Σῆρες, Seres, and who, no doubt, were the Chinese, and who were then, as now, celebrated for silken fabrics or seric stuff.

From seres comes the Latin *sericum*, the French *soie*, the German *seiden*, the Anglo-Saxon *seolc*, the Icelandic *silki*, and the English *silk*.

We are informed by Hawae-nan-tze, in a Chinese work called the "Silkworm

Classic," that Teling-she, the principal queen of Hwang-te, B.C. 2640, was the first to rear silkworms, and the Emperor Hwang-te was induced to invent robes and garments from this circumstance.

The queen and wives of the nobles through successive generations personally attended to the rearing of the silkworms. Alas! that, in these days of expediency, hurry, and greed, the faith in machinery should have so disastrously stifled the better faith in manipulation, both in silk handicraft work and the old love for the spinning wheel, to the detriment alike of all classes, from the noble to the low born, who have been robbed of much that in bygone days contributed to the comfort, occupation, and enjoyment, especially of the gentler sex. Surely here is a worthy object of reform for our national art schools. That this silk was of the mulberry-fed kind is evident from a further extract from the same work, which says, that afterwards "when Yu regulated the waters B.C. 2200, mention is made " in his work on the tribute of the land adapted for the mulberry tree having " been supplied with silkworms, from which time the advantage thereof gradually " increased." Horsfield and Moore's Catalogue, p. 377.

It is not known whether silk was utilised in India at so early a period as this; probably not; but that India learned the art from China is generally understood, although at what period is not known.

For more precise information respecting the westward spread of silk culture I would strongly recommend my hearers to read Dr. Birdwood's account in his handbook to the British India Section of the Paris Exhibition. This learned history of silk will be read with much pleasure by all who can see in silken stuffs something more than a mere commercial value. The account of its utilisation and spread from East to West is described with almost the charm of romance. Its development is traced from its earliest days in the East to its introduction at last into own own country in the reign of Henry VI., and again to those sad French times of the persecution of the religious Huguenots by Louis XIV., which drove their silk workers by a happy tide to our shores. How that tide has in our own times returned to France, and carried with it not the workers, but the industry, I leave for statesmen—and they have much to answer for—and manufacturers to think over and retrieve.

Europe may be said to have got hold of the silk industry by a fraud; two monks are said to have brought away the eggs from China concealed in their walking canes. A similar account is well related by Dr. A. Wallace of the way the eggs of the prized Yama-mai silkworm were abstracted from Japan by a young Japanese, who obtained them at the instigation of his European tutor at the risk of his life, for this was an offence there punishable by death. It would be but a small return for the benefits we have obtained to ourselves by these frauds if we could teach those weaker peoples the benefits of the better making, and above all the more friendly interchanging of stuffs and commodities. It is with this hope that I put the wild silk question before the Society of Arts, that, having India, with its extensive wild silk regions, in our possession, we may, by gentle means, teach the natives to improve the culture and preliminary stages of its manufacture; so that it may be brought from them in a state fit to be used by us for all the purposes of which, in its improved state, it is really capable, and, to use the words of Sir Louis Mallet in the first letter of instruction I received from the India Office, that "a new and very profitable industry may be founded in India."

The natural history of every kind of silk may be briefly stated to be this. From a small egg laid by the moth, of whatever species, appears in due season a small larva, or caterpillar, or worm, as it is usually called. This worm, after having lived its day, feeding only on the leaves of certain plants characteristic of its species, spins, or rather secretes, a fine thread of silk around itself, for covering and protection during the time it lies dormant in the next stage of its existence. As soon as it has secreted all the silk, it changes into a pupa or chrysalis, and remains inside its silken cell until the time comes for its appearance as an imago, or perfect insect, having four soft scaly wings, legs, and antennæ. When its hybernation is ended, it emits a fluid which softens the end of its cocoon cell, and, by means of its wing spines and legs, parts the fibres aside until the opening is large enough for it to creep out. After a short time its wings dry and expand, and it has entered into its perfect state. It lives only a few days in this phase of its existence. It is in this stage only that the race is perpetuated, the female laying a number of eggs, and dying soon afterwards.

Bombyx Mori.

What is generally known as the silk of commerce, in both ancient and modern days, is distinguished from all others by the singular circumstance of the larvæ which produce it feeding on the leaves of the mulberry tree. The moth is therefore named *Bombyx mori*.

It must not be inferred, however, that there is only one species, as is too generally thought. Mr. F. Moore assures me there is sufficient structural variation in moths which were at one time understood as *Bombyx mori* to constitute specific differences. The following species feed on the mulberry, and their silk is in ordinary and promiscuous use along with that of the *mori* :—

Bombyx sinensis (Hutton),
Bombyx crœsi (Hutton),
Bombyx fortunatus (Hutton),
Bombyx arracanenis (Hutton),
Bombyx textor (Hutton),

and no doubt several others not yet defined, but whose silk varies very much, such as that called Canton, and that called Tsatlee, although both are from China, as well as the silk from Japan, which has a thicker fibre than the Mori silk of other countries, being $\frac{1}{1650}$ of an inch thick, as against $\frac{1}{2100}$ of an inch of the Mori silk of Italy. The strength and tension of this and the wild silks, as well as the respective sizes of their cocoons, are given in the table of microscopic measurements which I have carefully revised for my lecture, confirming generally, but in several instances correcting, those I made for my monograph for the Paris Exhibition.

I have here some beautifully-prepared Italian silks of *B. Mori,* kindly lent to me for my paper by my friend M. H. Meyer, a large silk manufacturer at Milan.

The eggs of *Bombyx mori*, and the other species of *Bombyx*, form a most important article of commerce between Japan and Europe. They are imported from thence into Italy and the South of France annually, to supply the deficiency caused by the silkworm disease known as *pebrine*, and also to infuse, as it were, new blood. The value of the eggs is about 25*s*. per oz. Twelve pounds of cocoons are required to produce 1 lb. of silk. The value of the raw silk of Bengal in London is now 14*s*. 6*d*. per lb. The colour is generally of a rich golden yellow of this sample, but it is also sometimes white. In China and Japan it is all white, with rare exceptions.

Wild Silks.

As far as I can learn, the only species of cocoons at present utilised in India, besides those of the several species of mulberry-feeding worms of the genus *Bombyx*, are the wild ones of the following species :—

Attacus ricini,
,, cynthia,
,, atlas,
,, edwardsia,
Antheræa assama, or Munga worm,
,, paphia, or Tusser worm,
,, perotteti,
,, nebulosa,
,, roylei,
,, frithii,
,, mezankooria,
Circula trifenestrata,
And, perhaps,
Attacus selene and Antheræa helferi.

The India localities of the four principal ones, Ricini, Atlas, Munga, and Tusser, are shown on these maps by various colourings.

The Eria Silkworm.

We now arrive at the consideration of the Eria, Arindy, or Arundi worm, of which there are two species, *Attacus ricini* and *Attacus cynthia*. *Attacus ricini* (Boisd.) is known also under the names *Saturnia ricini* (Boisd.) and *Attacus lunula* (Walker).

Attacus ricini is a worm which feeds on the Palma christi, or castor-oil plant, *Ricinus communis.* It is a native of Assam, and, according to Mr. Geoghegan, is found to the south-west in a track comprising the districts of Nepaul, Kumaon, Ladak, Darjeeling, Dinagepore, Rungpore, and perhaps, parts of Bhangulpore, and Purmiah, and in Assam. In 1791, Sir W. Jones drew attention to this silk, and Dr. Roxburgh in 1804.

An official Report of the Government of India states that this worm in Assam spins a white silk, while in Dinagepore the colour of the cocoon, it is understood, is brown.

The leaves of the castor-oil plant, *Ricinus communis,* or Palma christi, are the best and commonest food, but it will also feed on the following :—Koosool, Hindoo grass, Murkurdal, Okonnee, Gomaree, Litta pakoree, Birzonally, *Xanthoxylon hostile, Coriaria nipalensis, Ailanthus glandulosa, Ailanthus excelsa.*

Attacus ricini is of a larger size than *Attacus cynthia*; owing probably to its freedom, and there is no doubt it is a silk producer of great importance in India. Probably the most complete account of it is by Mr. Geoghegan in his report on the silk industry of India, of which I avail myself to gather some useful particulars.

The *Attacus ricini*, according to Dr. Buchanan, feeds both on *Ricinus communis* and *Ricinus viridis.*

The female moth lays her eggs round a twig, and then dies. These twigs are sold in the markets covered with eggs, the dead moths frequently hanging to them, and presenting a very curious appearance.

The caterpillar moults four times, and when fully grown is about $3\frac{1}{2}$ inches long.

According to Mr. Hugon, the natives soften the cocoon in potash, and draw the silk off roughly with the finger and thumb, thus making a kind of spun silk. Dr. Buchanan, however, says the silk is wound on a reel in Dinagepore.

M. Guérin Méneville, however, stated in 1860 that it was impossible to reel this cocoon. I am certainly disposed to think it is quite impracticable. Still, there is a method of using it at hand, and I know of no silk better adapted for spinning.

Some of the cocoons I received from the India Office for examination I have had carded or dressed, and the result is, as is shown in this sample, a fibre of great fineness and length, which would be eagerly sought after by English and Continental spinners if the cocoons could be collected and sent over in quantity. Owing to the very small quantity of cocoons in my possession, I am sorry I have not been able to have specimens of yarn or cloth made for my lecture, but I have here native spun yarn undyed, bleached and dyed, also native woven cloth in the undyed and dyed states, as well as specimens of prints executed on it for, I believe, the first time in its history or use. The cloth is beautifully soft.

I find no difficulty in making this silk yield to tinctorial influences, either in dyeing or printing, and I have no hesitation in predicting a great future for it, as soon as it is subjected to the better spinning appliances of Europe, and I am recommending the Government of India to give all possible encouragement to the importation of Eria cocoons into Europe.

Dr. Helfer, in 1837, stated in the *Journal of the Asiatic Society of Bengal* that this worm is so productive as to give sometimes twelve broods of silk in the course of the year. The worm grows rapidly, and offers no difficulty whatever for an extensive speculation.

The industry of the natives of India should be stimulated to the gathering in of all kinds of wild silk cocoons, whether windable or not, for there is no doubt that those kinds which cannot be reeled can be most easily spun, and there is at the present moment a request on the part of silk spinners for a much larger supply of Tusser silk cocoons and Tusser silk waste for spinning purposes, and no doubt the other wild silk cocoons would be gladly bought up, especially those of *Attacus ricini.*

Mr. Geoghegan says, with regard to the thread from cocoons of *Attacus ricini,* that a seer of 96 sicca weight ($2\frac{464}{1000}$ lbs.) of this thread is worth from annas 12 (one shilling and sixpence) to Rs. 1 (two shillings), but it is very seldom sold, and the people who keep the insect in general rear no more than is just sufficient to make cloths for their own families. The cloth lasts very long, owing to which quality it is probable that some use might be found for this material in our manufactures at home.

Mr. Michael Atkinson, of Singapore, describes the cloth made of Eria to be of incredible durability, the life of one person being seldom sufficient to wear out a garment made of it, so that the same piece descends from mother to daughter.

The thickness of this fibre is $\frac{1}{1500}$ of an inch on the outside of the cocoon, and $\frac{1}{1430}$ in the inner part. (For other particulars *see* Table.)

TABLE OF THE DIAMETER, STRENGTH, AND TENSION OF A SINGLE FIBRE AND THE DIMENSIONS OF COCOON OF THE CHIEF MULBERRY AND INDIAN WILD SILKS.

Name of Worm and Silk.	Country.	Diameter in fractions of an inch.		Tension or limit of stretch before breaking in inches of single fibre one foot long.		Strength of single fibre in drams avoirdupois.		Dimensions of cocoons in inches.
		Outside of cocoon.	Inner part of cocoon.	Outside of cocoon.	Inner part of cocoon.	Outside of cocoon.	Inner part of cocoon.	
Bombyx mori, or Mulberry Silk.	China	$\frac{1}{2150}$	$\frac{1}{2150}$	1¼	1¾	2⅜	2⅞	1⅛ × ½
	Italy -	$\frac{1}{2150}$	$\frac{1}{2100}$	1	1¾	2⅝	2⅞	1¼ × ⅝
	Japan	$\frac{1}{1800}$	$\frac{1}{1650}$	1	1¾	2	2⅞	1⅛ × ⅝
	Bengal	$\frac{1}{2000}$	$\frac{1}{2200}$	1¼	1½	2⅛	2⅝	1¼ × ½
Bombyx textor - -	India -	$\frac{1}{2500}$	$\frac{1}{3800}$	1¼	1½	2¼	2½	1¼ × 1⅛
Antheræa paphia, or Tusser Silk.	,,	$\frac{1}{770}$	$\frac{1}{710}$	1	1	7	8	1½ × ⅞
Attacus ricini, or Eria Silk	,,	$\frac{1}{1500}$	$\frac{1}{1430}$	1	1½	1⅞	2⅛	1⅓ × ¾
Attacus cynthia, or Ailanthus Silk.	,,	$\frac{1}{1250}$	$\frac{1}{1250}$	1	1½	2¼	2½	1¾ × ¾
Antheræa assama, or Muga Silk.	,,	$\frac{1}{1480}$	$\frac{1}{1680}$	1	1¾	2⅛	3	1¾ × 1
Actias selene - -	,,	$\frac{1}{1000}$	$\frac{1}{1100}$	1	1¼	2	2¼	3 × 1¼
Attacus atlas - -	,,	$\frac{1}{1320}$	$\frac{1}{1000}$	1	1¼	2⅛	2½	3½ × ⅞
Antheræa yama-mai -	Japan	$\frac{1}{1000}$	$\frac{1}{1000}$	¾	1¾	2⅛	3	1½ × ⅞

An official report of the Government of India states that the natives of India use Eria silk for the manufacture of garments having the following names :— Borkapor, Meklas (petticoats), Rhiha (scarves), Goursha.

Mr. Hugon says that, "in Assam, the quantity of Eria cloth the merchants "formerly used to take away was very considerable, but in the latter years of the "Assam Rajah's rule, from the disorganised state of the country, the number of "merchants gradually diminished. The quantity the country is capable of exporting "under an improved management would be very large, for it forms at present the "dress of the poorer classes at all seasons, and is used by the highest for winter wear. "So long ago as 1769 vast quantities were being produced in the country around "Guraghaut." He estimated the annual production at 1,000 maunds, or 82,000 lbs. "In the district of Duriung the annual yield of Eria is 1,000 maunds, of which "one-third is exported either in the form of cocoons or woven into heavy cloths "(Borkapor)." Mr. Hugon stated that, for want of a proper solvent of the gum, the natives could not reel the cocoons. Mr. Brownlow states that in Cachar the Eria or Ricini worm is trained by the Cacharis, a people living in isolated villages on the hills. They soften the cocoons in a mixture of cow dung and water, and they are then carried off to a spindle by the women of the tribe. This silk is dyed by the natives with lac, mungeet, and indigo.

ATTACUS CYNTHIA.

Attacus cynthia (Drury).
Phalæna attacus cynthia (Drury).
Phalæna cynthia (Roxburgh).
Bombyx cynthia (Olivor).
Samia cynthia (Hübner).
Saturnia cynthia (Westwood).
Saturnia arrundi (Royle).
Eria of Assam (Hugon).

I have mentioned the close relationship of *Attacus cynthia* to *Attacus ricini*.

Mr. Geoghegan says *Attacus cynthia* occurs in a wild state throughout a great part of the Himalaya, in the Dehra Doon, and in Assam and Cachar.

In China *Attacus cynthia* feeds on the *Ailanthus glandulosa*. During the past 20 years much study has been bestowed on the species in Europe, and it has been successfully domesticated in France, and later on in England, so much so, that this study rejoices in the name Ailanthiculture, and the breeding-houses of the insect are called Ailantheries.

It is to M. Guérin-Méneville, in France, and to Lady Dorothy Neville, in England, that we are indebted for leading the way to the successful rearing of the *Attacus cynthia*. A description of their labours will be found in a memoir by Dr. Wallace, published in 1866, in the *Journal of the Entomological Society*. Besides giving full particulars of all that relates to Ailanthiculture, Dr. Wallace describes with great minuteness his own experience in producing this silk. He received the prize offered by the Council of the Society in 1865 for an essay on "Economic Entomology."

The diameter of all the fibres in the cocoon is tolerably uniform, and about $\frac{1}{1250}$ inch. The strength of the outer fibres is, however, only $2\frac{1}{4}$ drams, that of the inner being $2\frac{1}{2}$ drams. The tension of the outer fibres is one inch to the foot, and of the inner $1\frac{1}{2}$ inches. All the fibres are flat and longitudinally striated, and united in pairs by their edges. The cocoon is about the size of a thrush's egg, $1\frac{1}{2}$ to $2\frac{1}{4}$ inches long, and $\frac{3}{4}$ of an inch in diameter, and consists of very fine silk, laid together rather loosely, but closely. It offers great difficulty in winding, and I am not aware that this has yet been successfully accomplished, I mean commercially.

In 1864 Mr. Forgemol informed the Imperial Society of Acclimatisation, in France, of the particulars of a mode he had invented to reel this silk. Dr. Wallace has quoted this report, describing the method in his memoir. I fear, however, it it is not now in practical use. But whether the reeling has ever been done, or ever will be, there is no doubt that a great future remains for this silk, now that spinning machinery has been so perfected. All the cocoons that could be bred would be easily bought up by the silk spinners.

Attacus cynthia came originally to India from China. In 1856 cocoons were sent by Abbé Fantoni from the province of Shan-Tung in the north of China.

Successful breeding took place from these cocoons in Turin in 1857, and from these spring all those which have been since cultivated in France, England, and other European countries. Mr. Moore was the first to rear them in England in 1859.

Dr. Wallace gives a lengthened account of the tree on which *Attacus cynthia* best thrives, *Ailanthus glandulosa*, from which I extract the following interesting remarks :—

"The genus *Ailanthus* belongs to the family *Rutaceæ*, and to the tribe *Xanthoxyleæ*, or yellow woods. It is a large and beautiful tree, reminding us somewhat of the walnut. The leaf stalks are of great length ; some I have measured were three feet and a half to four feet long, pendant with a graceful curve at the lower third of their length ; the leaflets are large, some measuring eight and a half inches in length by three in breadth, from thirteen to seventeen on a leaf stalk ; near the base of the leaf the margin is toothed, and at the extremity of the tooth is a little gland, emitting a strong resinous odour, whence the name glandulosa ; of these teeth and glands there are generally two, three, or more on each leaflet. The same odour seems to be communicated more or less to the leaf, also to the larva, and in a less degree to the imago of *Attacus cynthia*."

The pupæ of this insect remain in the cocoon through the winter, except in those cocoons which are formed in the autumn, from which they emerge in three or four weeks. The remaining moths emerge in April, and pair in about 12 hours afterwards, and the female begins to lay her eggs almost immediately. The moths do not live long after their exit from the cocoon. About eight days is the duration of their existence in this last and perfect stage. The eggs of one female vary from 150 to 350; 30 of them weigh a grain. They hatch in 12 to 18 days, according to temperature. In seven days the tiny caterpillars complete their first stage by moulting, their second in five or six days after, being up to this time gregarious; their third moult occurs in another six days, and their fourth and last in six days more. By this time the larvæ are four inches long, and begin to spin their cocoons.

Attacus cynthia has two broods in the year.

Attacus Atlas.

The next silkworm to which I wish to draw your attention is the *Attacus atlas* of Linnæus, which is also known by the following names :—

Phalæna attacus atlas (Linn.).
Bombyx atlas (Fabricius).
Saturnia silhetica (Helfer).

The imago of this species is the largest of all the silk moths. As you will see in the case, it is a grand insect. It is called in France "Le Géant des Papillons." The largest specimens measure upwards of ten inches in expanse of wing. According to Horsfield it feeds on the melokka (*Phyllanthus emblica*), a plant known also in India as *Kupu gaga*. Mr. Geoghegan says this silkworm is found in Mussooree on the *Falconeria insignis, Bradleia ovata,* and other plants ; in Kumaon, on the barberry, where it is abundant, and also eastward to Cachar. Mr. Moore describes it as almost omnivorous. Mr. P. H. Gosse has just written a most interesting life-history of this species, describing all that is known of it. His paper, from which I quote a few pertinent facts, will be found in the *Entomologist* of February and March last. He says :—

"It is a widespread species, ranging over the south and east half of Asia, continental and insular; common on the slopes of the Himalayas, and all through India to the points of both peninsulas ; abundant in China ; scattered over the isles of the Archipelago, from Java to the Moluccas, to Borneo, and the Philippines, a range of 35° of latitude and 55° of longitude."

His efforts to breed the Atlas worm in England are described, and although he has not been very successful, owing to sickness and death in the larval stage, his account is very interesting. Captain Landy, of Surbiton, has succeeded in obtaining fifteen good cocoons from twenty-four eggs, the larvæ having been fed on the common barberry. Mr. Gosse has fed his on the sallow, others on the plum and apple-tree leaves. He states that all the family of *Saturniidæ* are very polyphagous.

An official report of the Government of India gives the following interesting list of plants on which the Atlas worm feeds ; quoted from an article in the Agri-Horticultural Society's Journal, by Mr. Brownlow, of Cachar :—

"1. Phakura (*Cinchonaceæ*).—Foliage slightly bitter, stature middling, tolerably abundant.

"2. No native name ; probably a laurel ; foliage redolent of prussic acid, fruit like a plum, kernel containing a large portion of oil, resembling that of bitter almonds ; stature large, not very common.

"3. Could not find out any native name, but the tree may easily be identified by its resemblance to the China tea plant, and its frequent occurrence as a weed in tea gardens, where it is often left by weeders by mistake for tea ; stature middling, common in jhum land, less so in primitive forest.

"4. Nagdana (*Artimisia sp.*?).—An annual and one of the most common of jhum weeds ; it may be known by the satin pile on its leaves, which rubbed with the fingers and smelt, cause sneezing ; they possess a scent similar to lavender. The Cachar name is quite local, and is probably given to it because of its fragrance. The true Nagdana is the *Boswellia thurifera* ; this plant is too small in stature to be available as a silk tree, for which in other respects its abundance peculiarly fits it.

"5. Monphul (*Cachar name*), known in Dacca as the Myna kata, a thorny rapid-growing fruit tree, not indigenous, but found in great quantities self-sown about the villages ; the fruit is somewhat smaller than an apple, but, except in being yellow, has a good deal of resemblance to that fruit ; the fruit is cut up by the natives into slices, which are threaded on a string and hung up in their houses to smoke and dry ; stature middling.

"6. Balos, a rapid-growing weed which affects new clearances ; the deep green of the leaf, with the elongated delicate red leaf stalks, enable it to be easily recognised ; very common and of large stature ; fed on also by A. Canningi.

"7. Koorkooree, one of the commonest of jhum weeds ; it invades and monopolises large tracts of land, exclusively, or very nearly so ; grows to a middling stature, and where abundant, shades the ground completely. This tree is one of the most eligible for training the Atlas on.

"8. Lutki (*Osbeckia*), the common conspicuous pink-flowering plant ; it scarcely grows large enough to train silk on, but the silk from worms fed on it is very white.

"9. Bon Chelita ; so called from a resemblance in the grouping of the leaves to the Chelita ; a large hardy rapid-growing tree, sufficiently common for purposes of silk cultivation.

"10. Kadam (*Nauclea*), a common large leaved rapid-growing tree, especially on new clearings, where it soon, if allowed to grow, overshades the land ; well adapted as a nurse for young tea, or any delicate plants ; the leaves become of great size when the plant is young, especially on rich hill lands ; as the tree grows larger they diminish in size ; occurs mostly on hill lands, seldom on alluvial.

"11. Chelita (*Dillenea speciosa*), a large-sized luxuriant tree, partial to alluvial lands, on which it may be found in clumps or groves; grows very well, even in badly-drained soil, and with water about the roots; owing to the large size of this tree, its growing in clusters, and the large quantity and bushiness of its foliage, it is eminently adapted for training the Atlas worm on.

"12. Boidraj (*Padrelacæ*?), a large sized and very common tree in old forests. Atlas silk of this is very dark. This tree is very common in the Sylhet district, and occurs all the way down to Dacca.

"13. Lood, also a full-sized tree, may be known by its dark green shiny leaves and its bark, which is thicker than that of, probably, any other tree; this tree is also fed on by the A. Canningi."

It is interesting to observe the micaceous or window-like spot on each of the four wings. These, although characteristic of the *Saturniidæ* are almost more largely developed in *Attacus atlas* than in any other species. The French call these vitreous membranes *porte miroirs*.

There are several varieties of *Attacus atlas* which show their divergence from the type by the variations of these fusiform window-like ornamentations. In some they are single, in others double.

The diameter of the external fibres of the cocoon is very variable, averaging about $\frac{1}{1320}$ inch, whilst that of the internal fibres is more uniform, and about $\frac{1}{1000}$ inch. The outer fibres are capable of supporting an average weight of $2\frac{1}{8}$ drams, and the inner $2\frac{1}{2}$ drams. The tension of the outer fibres is one inch to the foot, and the inner $1\frac{1}{4}$ inches. The fibres are flat and longitudinally striated, and united in pairs by their edges.

The egg of *Attacus atlas* is $\frac{8}{100}$ of an inch long. The larvæ moult six times. The cocoon of *Attacus atlas* is from two to three inches long, and about one inch wide at the widest part, and weighs two grammes, or the $\frac{1}{14}$th of an ounce.

Mr. Gosse says, "the colour of the cocoon is a light umber or drab; its surface (independently of the impress of leaves) roughly granular, scarcely at all silky or floccose, except at the mouth; its substance thin, parchmenty, very firm; the interior very smooth, and even sub-glossy. The upper extremity forms a natural orifice for the exit of the moth, made by the conveyance of a great number of silk-fibres, which are left ungummed, and are thus soft and flossy, the gummed stiff silk passing up on one side, and contracting into the cord. Thus the cocoon is not closed, like those of *Bombyx mori*, of *Telea*, of the *Antheræa*, but open, like those of *A. cynthia*, of the *Samiæ*, of the *Saturniæ*. As a result of this structure, the exit of the imago leaves no disturbance behind, no witness, no disarrangement of these soft fibres, such as is the case with Yama-mai, Pernyi, and Mylitta.

Mr. Geoghegan states the silk to be difficult to reel, though it reels partially if boiled with vinegar. Captain Hutton says the silk is decidedly good, and Dr. Chavannes, of Lausanne, states it to be desirable of introduction into France. He says the worm is the Fagara of China, where it has long been cultivated.

Attacus Edwardsia.

In the Indian Museum there are two specimens of an atlas moth, from Darjeeling, of an intensely dark colour, and possessing sufficient structural divergence from *Attacus atlas* to warrant Mr. Moore's affirming it to be a distinct species. It has been named *Attacus Edwardsia*. Mr. Gosse has the following interesting note respecting it:—

"As Darjeeling is 7,000 feet above the sea, and has a climate in which rain and snow are abundant in winter, and humidity is constant, it surely would not be difficult to acclimatise this noble form (be it variety or species) in the British Isles."*

The Moonga, Mooga, or Muga Silk.

I have here a silk produced from the worm known as the *Moonga*, or *Mooga*, *Antheræa assama* (Helfer), and *Saturnia assama* (Westwood). It is found in Assam, and also sparingly in the Dehra Doon, and is the next in importance to tusser. Mr. Geoghegan's description of this silk occupies three pages of the Blue-book on the silk industry of India, from which I abstract the following particulars:—

"The worm that gives the common fawn-coloured moonga silk, when fed on the

* Gosse's "Life History of *Attacus atlas*," p. 6.

most common plants, gives a whitish silk when fed on the leaves of other silk-worm plants. The plants it feeds on are named and estimated as follows :—

"No. 1. *Champa* (*Michelia*).—The silk produced from the worm feeding on this plant gives the finest and whitest silk, used only by the rajah and great people, and is called champa pattea moonga. The thread is sold at from 11 to 12 rupees a seer (11*s*. to 12*s*. per lb.).

"No. 2. *Maizankurry* (called also addakurry).—The old trees are cut down and the jungle about burnt, and the worms are fed upon the tender leaves of the off-shoots for one year, when the leaves become too old and hard for the worms. Silk is sold at 6 to 7 rupees per seer (6*s*. to 7*s*. per lb.).

"The silk from worms fed by the Maizankurry plant is rare, and is produced in Sibsagar, Assam. Although a variety of Muga silk, it is generally known as Mezankuri silk.

"No. 3. *Soom*.—This is the common tree of the vicinity; the silk from the worms fed on this gives the finest sort of fawn-coloured moonga. Silk is sold at 3½ to 4 rupees per seer (3*s*. 6*d*. to 4*s*. per lb.).

"No. 4. *Soonhalloo* (*Tetranthera macrophylla*).—This is also a brown silk of inferior quality. This plant is most common in Dhurumpore and about Russa Chokey.

"No. 5. *Digluttee* (*Tetranthera diglottica*).—This is also brown silk of inferior quality, but the worms fed on the leaves of this tree increase much in size.

"No. 6. *Pattees hoonda* (*Laurus obtusifolia*).

"The moonga worm also feeds on the Kontooloa. The botanical name of Soom is *Machilus odoratissima*.

"The moonga worm gives broods five times a year, and the cocoon is very large, but thin. I could only obtain silk, the produce of worms feeding on Nos. 3 and 4, and manufactured into cheap cloths for the lower classes.

"In its natural fawn-colour it stands washing much better than ordinary silk, keeping gloss and colour till the last."*

Mr. Geoghegan, on page 114 of his "Silk Industry of India," says :—

"The cycle of the insect is thus given :—

From emergence from the egg to commencement of cocoon - - - - -	30 days.
In the cocoon - - - -	20 "
As a moth - - - - -	6 "
In the egg - - - - -	10 "
Total - - -	66 days."

In 1873, Colonel Hopkinson, the Commissioner of Assam, gave more modern figures :—

"It thence appears that the soom forests (on which the worm is chiefly fed) cover an area of about 34,000 acres, of which about 18,000 are assessed, yielding a revenue of nearly Rs. 28,000 (2,800*l*.). By far the greater portion of the assessed area lies in the district of Sibsagar. The production of the silk is said to employ some 48,000 persons, but it is not their sole calling. The out-turn of silk is estimated at upwards of 100,000 lbs. But as it is admitted that the greater part of the silk is reserved for home manufacture, this estimate cannot be regarded as absolutely trustworthy. The price of the yarn per seer (2 lbs.) varies from Rs. 5 (10*s*.) to Rs. 9 (18*s*.) in the several districts. The small portion exported goes to Calcutta and Dacca. From the former place it is said to find its way, to some extent, to Bhangulpur and Bombay.

"The Silk Committee of the Agri-Horticultural Society reported favourably on some munga silk sent down by Captain Jenkins in 1839, and expressed their opinion that the article was calculated to become of extensive and valuable use to our home manufactures."*

One acre of land yields 50,000 Muga silk cocoons, which yield upwards of twelve seers (24 lbs.) of silk, price Rs. 5 per seer, or 5*s*. per lb.

From Mr. Hugon's description of the mode of reeling it is evident it is of the rudest kind, and points to a remedy in the improved Continental reeling appliances.

The following particulars by Mr. Hugon in 1834 are interesting :—The Muga silk industry is confined to Assam and some Tipperah villages. The quantity of

* Geoghegan, "Silk Industry of India," p. 25.

land planted with food for the muga was 5,000 acres, capable of yielding 1,500 maunds (123,000 lbs.) of silk. This silk formed one of the principal exports of Assam. The average quantity was 257 maunds (21,070 lbs.) valued at Rs. 56,054 (5,605*l.*), leaving the country principally in the shape of thread. He advocates the use of the moonga silk in coloured fabrics, it being easily dyed.

An Official Report of the Government of India states that the natives of India use Muga silk for making fabrics and garments known by the following names :—

Soorias (dhoties).
Meklas (petticoats).
Jootha Borakapor (worn in winter).
Rhiha (scarves).
Chhelan (for men's shoulders).
Mashris (curtains).

Having only a very small quantity of coarse reeled Muga silk at my disposal, my experiments with it have been limited. I find it bleaches well, is very lustrous, and takes the dye freely, better than Tusser. Here are specimens of it in the raw, boiled-off, bleached, and dyed states, and also some waste from cocoons for spinning.

The diameter of the fibres of Muga silk taken from the external part of the cocoon averages $\frac{1}{1430}$ inch, but the external fibres are very variable. The diameter of the inner and less variable fibres is $\frac{1}{1080}$ inch. The outer fibres will break with a weight of $2\frac{1}{8}$ drams on the average, but the inner will support three drams. The tension of the outer fibres averages one inch to the foot, and of the inner $1\frac{3}{4}$ inches. All the fibres are like Tusser, flat and striated, and united in pairs by their edges.

The following table is given by Mr. Hugon, showing the nature and prices of the various kinds of cloth made from Moonga silk :—

Name of Cloth.	Size of Yards and Inches.	Weights.		Price of Thread.		Cost of Weaving.		Total.		Remarks.
		lbs.	ozs.	*s.*	*d.*	*s.*	*d.*	*s.*	*d.*	
Goovias - -	4 × 30 in.	0	12	3	9	0	$4\frac{1}{2}$	4	$1\frac{1}{2}$	Dhoties.
Ditto - -	9 × 1–4 in.	2	0	10	0	1	0	11	0	Dhoties.
Mekla - - -	$2\frac{3}{4}$ × 1	0	8	2	6	0	3	2	9	Petticoats.
Rhia - -	$6\frac{3}{4}$ × $\frac{3}{4}$	1	0	5	0	0	6	5	6	Scarves.
Gaursha - -	$4\frac{1}{2}$ × 20 in.	0	4	1	3	0	$1\frac{1}{2}$	1	$4\frac{1}{2}$	Worn as turbans or round the waist.
Joonta Bor Cappor	$6\frac{3}{4}$ × $1\frac{1}{4}$	2	0	4	0	0	9	4	9	Made of the floss, and worn in winter.

Antheræa Perotteti.

This is described by Mr. Geoghegan as producing a strong, wiry, and brilliant silk, but requires carding. The larvæ feed, in captivity, on the *Odina wodier* (Roxb.). "Undergoes four moults, and yields four crops a year." Fishing lines of this silk are said to be made in Dinapoor.

Antheræa Roylei.

Is described by the same author as being found at Darjeeling, and in the Himalayas from Kumaon to the Punjaub, and feeds on *Quercus incana.* The silk is good, but not abundant, and the insect can be domesticated. Yields two or three crops a year.

Tusser Silk.

I now come to the principal subject of my paper, the Tasar silk, called also Tusser, Tusseh, Tussah, Tussore. It is the product of the larvæ of the moth *Antheræa paphia* of Linnæus. It is known by the following synonyms* :—

Phalæna attacus paphia (Linnæus).
Bombyx paphia (Fabricius).
Phalæna paphia (Roxburgh).
Saturnia paphia (Helfer).

* Horsfield and Moore's Catalogue of Lepidopterous Insects, p. 385.

Phalæna attacus mylitta (Drury).
Bombyx mylitta (Fabricius).
Antheræa mylitta (Hübner).
Attacus mylitta (Blanchard).
Saturnia mylitta (Westwood).
Bugby silkworm moth of the Burbhoon hills.
Kolisurra silkworm moth of the Mahrattas.

There is but little doubt that this silk has been utilised for many centuries, both in India and China, but I have not been able to find any account of its Eastern history.

For the history and other particulars of Tusser silk I am glad to acknowledge my indebtedness to the report of Mr. Geoghegan. He attributes the derivation of the word Tusser to *tusuru*, the Hindostani for shuttle, and states this caterpillar to be the most widely distributed, as well as the most important, of the wild silk producers of India.

It is elsewhere stated that in the Central Provinces cloth is made of cotton warp and tusser weft, so in this case tusser silk would be the weft silk or shuttle silk.

One of the earliest notices of this insect, or of a species very nearly related to it, is given in the "Herbarium Amboinense" by the venerable Rumphius, who was born at Hanau in 1657 (dedicated by him to the East India Company), vol. III., page 113, pl. 75; he discovered the larvæ in Amboina feeding on the *Mangium caseolari rubrum* (Rizophora caseolaris, Linn.), a plant of the order of Terebintaceæ."* He says:—

"When I had kept the cocoons for three weeks, a moth came out quite perfect, which was the most beautiful and largest I had ever seen, which, biting away (the silk), showed its head, and at the same time drew out with it a little flock of yellow silk; this the moth performed at night. Its body, like all other moths, is a dirty yellow colour, and in length two joints of a finger; it has two downy horns on its head, of a golden hue, and four large wings, of which the two largest are about an inch long and of a golden colour, but a purple line runs through them transversely, and every wing has, as it were, in its middle a window-like eye, which is surrounded by a purple circle, and, as it were, of the transparency of glass."

The larvæ, when fully grown, are about four inches in length; they have twelve joints or articulations, besides their extremities; their colour is green, resembling the leaves on which they feed; and they are marked with reddish spots, and a reddish-yellow band running lengthways. They feed on several plants:—

Rhizophora calceolaris (Linn).
Terminalia alata glabra (Assum tree).
Terminalia tomentosa (the saj tree).
Terminalia catappa (country almond tree).
Tectona grandis (teak tree).
Zizyphus jujuba (ber tree).
Shorea robusta (sal tree).
Bombax heptaphyllum (Semul).
Careya sphærica.
Pentaptera tomentosa.
Pentaptera glabra.
Ricinus communis (castor-oil plant).
Cassia lanceolata.

In six weeks from the time they are hatched they begin to spin their cocoons, which they most curiously suspend from the branches of the trees, by constructing a thick hard cord or pedicle of silky matter, which is made to grasp the branches, as seen in these specimens.

Tusser silk is found, as you will see by the map, over nearly the whole of India.

In the Central Provinces, Mr. Geoghegan says, Tusser is utilised in Rajpore, Bilaspore, Sumbulpore, the Upper Godavery, Chanda, Bhundora, Nagpore, Balaghab, Seonee, Chindwara, Betool, and Nursinghpore. Sumbulpore is said to yield 3,500 seers (7,000 lbs.) of silk; Rajpore, 6,000 (12,000 lbs.); Bilaspore, 900 (1,800 lbs.); and Chanda, 22,500 (45,000 lbs.) The silk is woven and used in the provinces in mixed fabrics of cotton woof and Tusser weft. But, at any

* Horsfield and Moore's Catalogue of Lepidopterous Insects, pp. 386–7.

rate, in some districts, muktahs, garments worn by Brahmins after bathing, cholees, women's bodices, and doputtas and dorwas, seem to be made of pure Tusser silk.

Captain Brooke* says :—

"In Seonee there is a regularly organised and thoroughly understood industry, from the rearing of the insects to the weaving of silk into cloth, with all its accompanying machinery of trade guilds, money-lenders, &c. This state of things is, in my opinion, no disadvantage; for, in place of having to contend with the difficulties which, in India, always surround the introduction of anything new or unknown, the demand is all that is necessary to stimulate production to any extent required. Nor is this a figure of speech, for the natural food of the Tussar worm is the leaves of the saj, lendeya, and dhowra trees, all of which are found in every part of this district, and are, I believe, common to the whole of Gondwana. These trees are, besides, propagated with facility, and, as far as the requirement of the silk insect goes, are of rapid growth; hence, if the silk became more known and better valued, and the profits sufficiently attractive, we might witness a development of the culture similar in kind to that which has of late years taken place in the case of cotton. Supposing, then, a demand to spring up, I am of opinion that the supply would, in a very short time, amply meet it. The nucleus of no inconsiderable trade now exists, and only awaits the stimulus of high prices. The primary question whether the product is, or may become, of such value as to occasion a large demand, is one, perhaps, that more nearly concerns traders than Indian administrations; still, so convinced am I of the value and beauty of the fabric that can be woven from well-reeled Tasar, that I would venture to strongly urge Government action in introducing it to the markets of Europe."

The worms require protection from birds and ants, which are their greatest enemies. The first cocoons are made in August, and are sold, after the moth has escaped, to the silk dealers at 4 to 8 pice (1½*d.* to 3*d.*) the hundred. The unpierced cocoons are only sold to rearers as seed, at 1·8 rupees to 2 rupees (3*s.* to 4*s.*) per hundred.

Captain Brooke says, "In Chanda and Bilaspoor, Central Provinces, the rearing "of the worms is attended by many ceremonial observances, which begin when the "insect leaves the egg, and are not discontinued until the cocoons are gathered "and taken to the rearer's house. During the feeding of the worm the Dheemurs "lead lives of the strictest abstinence. None of the sex are allowed within a "considerable distance of the trees upon which the worms are feeding, and if by "chance a woman or impure man passes near the feeding grounds, the trees and "worms are sprinkled in the name of Iogni (an incarnation of the god Mahadeo, "whom the worms are supposed to represent) with water taken, if procurable, "from a running stream, and in which tulsi leaves have been steeped. During "the same period the Dheemurs carefully abstain from flesh, fish, or haldi as their "food, nor do they cut their hair or shave, and carefully deny themselves all "ablution. When the cocoons are formed, they collect into a heap, and a goat, "pig, or fowl is sacrificed to Mahadeo in his form Iogni, the blood is sprinkled "over the cocoons, and, after a bout of liquor, are taken home. On the third day "following the Dheemurs shave and resume their normal condition."†

The caterpillars moult five times, at intervals of from five to eight days. When first hatched they weigh but ⅕th of a grain, and are about ¼ inch long; but at the end of their larval existence, which is from forty to forty-five days, they have attained a size of seven inches long, one inch in diameter, and weigh about 370 grains. Then they begin to spin their cocoons, which are, as you see, of an egg shape, and silvery drab in colour. The silk is all regularly deposited in a compact manner, resembling in thickness and substance the shell of an egg.

The cocoons vary much in size. The largest I have seen are from Sambulpoor, and are two inches long and 1¼ inches in diameter, whilst smaller ones are not more than 1⅛ inches long and ⅝ inch in diameter. The weight of the large cocoons is, without the pupa and supporting pedicle, 28 grains; the smaller ones 8 grains. I have here an unbroken double thread reeled for me, from one cocoon, by Mr. H. Meyer, of Milan. It weighs 12 grains, and measures 1,332 yards, or a little more than three-quarters of a mile.

---

* Geoghegan, "Silk Industry of India," p. 109.

† Captain Brooke, as quoted in Geoghegan, "Silk Industry of India," p. 110.

Mr. Coussmaker remarks* :—

"As a rule, there are certainly two crops in the year; the moths of the first batch come out in about four or six weeks after the first lot of worms (which come out at the commencement of the rains) have spun; those of the second batch remain quiescent until the rains begin again, that is to say, until May. As this entails the chrysalis remaining in the cocoon as long as eight months, exposed to the hottest sun and occasional thunderstorms, the cocoon had need to be made of a hard impenetrable material; so indestructible is it that Bheels, and other tribes which live in the jungles, use the cocoon as an extinguisher to the bamboo tube in which they keep the "falita," or cotton-rope tinder, used by them for lighting their tobacco and the slow matches of their matchlocks. The cocoon is also cut into a long spiral band, and used for binding the barrel of the matchlock to the stock, being, as the natives say, unaffected either by water or fire. The cocoon consists of two kinds of silk; what it first spins is reddish, and of this the pedicle and outside network is made. This silk consists of threads of different lengths, but the rest is generally unbroken from beginning to end. . . . After the caterpillar has spun a layer of silk thick enough to conceal itself, it discharges some kind of gum or cement, thick and white, like plaster of Paris, and then, with its muscular action, it causes the gum to thoroughly permeate the whole cocoon and solidify the wall. In this manner it goes on, spinning layer after layer of loops, and cementing them all together until the whole of its silk is exhausted, and the wall of the cocoon becomes so hard that it requires a sharp penknife to cut through it. The ring at the end of the pedicle, which has been spun round the twig, is a most necessary provision of nature, for it often happens that either the caterpillar has been unable to attach its cocoon to a leaf, or that, during the long time the cocoon remains unburst in the tree, the leaf or leaves to which the cocoon was at first attached become separated from it, and then the cocoon hangs suspended to the twig like a berry."

After eight or nine months in the pupa state, a moist spot is observed at one end of the cocoon. The moth is now about to emerge both from its pupa shell and from the cocoon. It secretes a fluid, which softens the cement of the cocoon, and enables it to separate the fibres sufficiently to allow its creeping out, it being, no doubt, assisted in this by its short pointed spines. Prof. Church is at present engaged in the investigation of the nature of this softening fluid. The head of the moth first appearing with its antennæ, broad in the male and narrow in the female, thus enabling the observer to note the sex, and to put them in pairs. The male moth generally flies away the night of his exit from the cocoon, after his wings become extended and dried. The female rarely does, but during the first three days of her existence she lays her eggs, which hatch in about twelve days afterwards. The new life of the moth does not extend to more than eleven days. As you will see from the specimens in the case, the moth is a fine and handsome insect, measuring across the wings about six inches in the male, and about five inches in the female. You will notice the similar vitreous and transparent wing spots to those of the Atlas moth. These spots are regarded with superstitious reverence by the natives, who see in them a resemblance to the chakra or discus of the god Vishnu, and are therefore induced to consider the moth a sacred insect.†

The latest report on Tusser culture is one from Major Coussmaker, dated Jangaon, Ahmednagar, on the 10th of January of the present year.

At Poonah he has established a breeding establishment, and has planted many young trees for feeding the worm. He says it thrives well on *Lagerstræmia indica*, an ornamental shrub fairly abundant in the cantonment of Poonah. He has changed his plan of feeding them on cut twigs brought to them in captivity, and allows them, carefully watched, to feed in the open air on the growing shrubs. This was an evident change for the better; the larvæ moulted in four to five days instead of five to eight days; they spun their cocoons in 28 to 35 days instead of from 40 to 50 days, and the moths emerged from the cocoons in 27 to 30 days, their eggs proving more fertile than under the former plan. He fed them also on *Carissa carandus*, and they throve still better on this; but the *Lagerstræmia*, after having all its leaves eaten off, being cut off and repotted, was in thick leaf again in a fortnight, and was ever sprouting, whilst the *carissa* did not sprout again after having been once denuded.

* "The Tusser silkworm," p. 9, 1873.

† Geoghegan.

For the next season's experiments Major Coussmaker has planted between 700 and 800 plants of the following species: *Lagerstræmia indica, Lagerstræmia parviflora, Conocarpus latifolia, Carissa carandus, Zizyphus jujuba*, and *Pentaptera tomentosa*, so that we may look forward with a large degree of interest to the result of so practical an experiment to domesticate this interesting silk producer in the Deccan.

Capt. Brooke says*:—

"In Chanda and Sunboolpoor, Central Provinces, when the cocoon crop is gathered, koshtas, a weaving caste, visit the village and buy them from the rearers. They are then, as soon as practicable, boiled in a lye made from the ashes of Jungni stalks, a plant grown for the oil expressed from its seed. This process effectually kills the chrysalis, at the same time dissolving the mucilage of the cocoon. The cocoons are then stored for use. The method of reeling is primitive in the extreme, and to its imperfections I solely attribute the scant attention this valuable and very beautiful silk has hitherto received. A description of the process is as follows:—The spinner, always a woman, sits on the ground. On her left is an earthen vessel with a thickish rim, about 6 in. in diameter and 3 in. deep. The saucer is three parts filled with a mixture of potash and ashes, patted down to a level surface, and kept damp with water. Upon this the cocoons to be spun are placed, the outer portion, of inferior and nearly useless silk, having been first removed. The thread in ordinary use amongst the weavers is spun from seven cocoons. These are all placed at the same time in the earthen saucer, a filament is then taken up from each cocoon, and, being brought together, are rolled between the hand and left thigh of the spinner, which are kept damp by an acid solution of tamarind and water."

In Bengal the cocoons are put into boiling water to kill the pupæ. In some districts, when intended for sale, they are put in boiling water and dried in the sun. In the Nizam's country the cocoons are loaded with dhobee's earth and alkaline ashes to make the reel. In the Midnapore district they are boiled in cow-dung, and reeled by hand.

Major Coussmaker, in a letter to me from Bombay, suggests the plan of placing the cocoons inside an earthenware jar, sealing it hermetically, and immersing it for an hour in a vessel of boiling water, and by this process the pupæ are killed by dry hot air. He thinks, however, that with this process the chrysalides will not be easy to dessicate, as they are so large and contain so much fatty or oily matter—the lubricating material required for the machinery of the moth's life—the *Antheræa* being one of that class which does not feed in its perfect state. After having killed the pupæ in this way, Major Coussmaker placed half his cocoons out daily in the sun for nine days and the other half let dry indoors, but still was not able to prevent the putrefaction of the pupæ, which of course depends on the moisture left in it, and causes the bad smell so common to Tusser silk in its raw state. He says if the drying operation is conducted in an oven the difficulty is to prevent the cocoons from being burnt, and if they are put on shelves under cover they are destroyed by beetles and ants, and that thus cages of perforated zinc or wire gauze will have to be resorted to, and so make the process expensive, and put the work out of the reach of the poorer classes. He says: "I am afraid I can see nothing "before us but a plantation and a drying shed on a large scale. We have "certainly the indigenous insect and its food and cheap labour at hand, but "careful, and of course expensive, superintendence and careful preparation are "required, and at first this will raise the price of the article, but with patience "and perseverance we shall get it down to its proper level."

Capt. Brooke says that, in Seonee, the pierced cocoons are wound, and that no koshtee rejects a cocoon simply because the moth has eaten its way through it. He has fallen into an error as to the moth's mode of exit from its cocoon. It separates the fibres with its legs and wing spines, and so creeps out. It has neither teeth nor mouth proper.

Each species of silkworm has two stores of silk, one on each side of the alimentary canal, and below its mouth it has two so-called spinnarets or orifices, through which the silk issues simultaneously in fine parallel filaments. As the silk

* Geoghegan, "Silk Industry of India," p. 111.

is drawn out of the stores the worm coats it with a varnish, technically called gum, which contains a brownish yellow colouring matter.

The Tusser worm, in spinning his cocoon, takes short sweeps of his head from side to side, depositing the silk very closely in parallel fibres as he does so. It has been thought that the worm twists the silk as it exudes it, but this is not the case. Besides the gum which coats the silk, the worm secretes at intervals a cementing fluid, which it kneads by an expanding motion of its body through the whole cocoon to consolidate and harden it. This cement gives to the cocoon its drab colour.

There is a striking peculiarity about the fibre of Tusser silk. I have carefully and thoroughly examined it many times under the microscope, and find undoubtedly that the fibre is flat and not round, like mulberry silk.

There is no doubt that it is to this property that Tusser silk owes its glassy or vitreous look, reflecting a little glare of light from the angle of incidence on its flat surface, whilst the mulberry silk fibre, being round, reflects the light equally in all directions.

By some this property is considered a drawback, but by the time the fibre has become modified, and the flatness diffused in the loom, I think the lustre of the cloth is enhanced by it.

This tape-like appearance gives the fibre this disadvantage, that it is less homogeneous than the round fibre of the mulberry silk, and I find an undoubted tendency in it to split up into smaller fibrets, thus causing the silk to swell out when subjected to severe dyeing processes, particularly the bleaching one of recent date, thus giving a substantial and important reason why its coloured cements should be removed by gentle action.

The fibrets have a distinct structure, upwards of twenty in number, and seem compactly laid together, showing the striated longitudinal appearance of the fibre under the microscope. I daresay it is this fibrous compound structure, absent, as you see, in the mulberry fibre, which is an element in its dye-resisting power. I found permanganate of potash to be the best agent to separate these fibrets.

I have now had fibres of Tusser silk immersed in alcohol, ether, permanganate of potash (acidified with sulphuric acid), dilute acids, and alkalis for about ten months without any satisfactory result in separating the fibres, except in the case of permanganate of potash, which in so long a time dissolves or carbonizes the silk, but prior to doing so, separates the fibrets to some considerable extent in a few days.

The diameter from edge to edge of a single flat fibre of Tusser silk from the outer part of the cocoon averages $\frac{1}{770}$ part of an inch, and from deeper in the substance of the cocoon $\frac{1}{710}$ of an inch, but the external fibres are much more variable than the internal. The thickness from side to side is $\frac{1}{1900}$ of an inch. The outside fibres are capable of supporting, without breaking, an average weight of seven drams, and the inner eight drams, whilst the usual amount of tension in all the fibres is one inch to the foot. The fibres, like all other silk fibres, are laid in the cocoon by the silkworm in pairs, united by their edges, and not by their flat surfaces.

All the *Saturniidæ* fibres I have examined are more or less fibrous and flat, except the English species *Saturnia carpini*, or Emperor moth, which, in North Staffordshire, spins a beautiful cocoon in the heather of our moorlands. My son has drawn for me an enlarged microscopic appearance of this silk, which shows its transparent and fibretless nature; and also, what is very curious, that the fibres are round except where they come in contact, when they become flat, no doubt from pressure. This apparent exception to the *Saturniidæ* depositing flat fibres and the *Bombycidæ* round ones, which I had established, possibly points to the secretion of the sericene in the different species varying in fluidity, that of the *Saturniidæ* being excreted in a more fluid state than that of the *Bombycidæ*. There may also be a difference in the structure of their seripositors; but this I have not had an opportunity of investigating.

In an Official Report of the Government of India the following table is given as the life-history of several of the chief silk-producing worms :—

Name of Silkworm.	Period of Life of Moth.	Period from laying of Eggs to their being Hatched.	Period of Life of the Worm.	Period from beginning of Worm to Spin to Completion of Chrysalis.	From Completion of Chrysalis to Emergence of Moth from Cocoon.
I. Tasar or Kutkuri -	3 or 4 days	9 days	36 days	15 days	Not given
II. Moonga - -	6 days	10 days	30 days	5 or 6 days	10 to 20 days
III. Eria or Arindi -	Not known exactly		A complete cycle is made in from 43 days to 2 months.		
IV. Pat major (Bombyx textor) - - } Pat minor (Bombyx crœsi) - - }	3 or 4 days	10 months	30 to 40 days	5 or 6 days	20 to 25 days
Attacus Atlas - -	No exact details are given		Eggs lie dormant through cold weather, and two, or perhaps three, crops are obtained in the year.		

In the same report are given the following statements :—

" The Pat gives only one crop of cocoons in the year.

" In Upper Assam the eggs of the Pat are hatched about the end of December.

" In Lower Assam the eggs of the Pat are hatched about the end of January.

" The Eria sometimes gives as many as seven crops in the year, and the Muga gives five crops a year.

" The difference in colour of cocoons in the case of cocoons of the same silkworm is known to be due partly to the local influence of climate and largely to the food which the silkworm eats.

" Of wholly domesticated worms the common kinds in Assam are the Pat major and the Pat minor, and the Eria or Arundy. Both these kinds of silkworms are fed within doors, the leaves of the trees and the plants they feed upon being plucked and brought to them. The Pat (Bombyx textor) which is closely allied to the common mulberry silkworm (Bombyx mori) of Europe is more delicate, and has to be treated with more care than the Eria. The silk of the Pat is, however, more valuable. Great care has to be taken to keep everything about the Pat scrupulously clean.

" A general point to observe in silkworm rearing is that silkworms of as nearly as possible the same size and strength only should be allowed to feed together. If this rule be not observed the stronger silkworms will bully the weaker, and deprive the latter of their food.

" The chief partially domesticated silkworms of the Province of Assam are the Muga, the Tasar, and the Attacus Atlas. The two latter are also found in a wholly wild state, and a silkworm, probably the same as the Muga of Assam, is found wholly wild in Cachar. Some of the other wild silkworms of this province are said to have been partially domesticated. In Assam the Muga may be said to be wholly domesticated, but in its general treatment corresponds to the Tasar and Atlas, and other wild silkworms which have been at times partially domesticated, and it is convenient, therefore, to consider the Muga as of this partially domesticated class.

" The difference in treatment of this class of silkworms consists in this, that they are fed out of doors and not kept within houses. The Muga eggs are laid on small bundles of grass or straw, half the thickness of a finger, and tied to the trees before they are hatched. The Muga worms are reared on the trees, and standing in the open, and not on leaves collected and given to the worms in houses, as in the case with Pat and Eri. Great care has to be taken to destroy the ants, which would otherwise kill the silkworm. This is frequently done by putting baits of molasses, fish, or dead toads at the foot of the tree. But, besides these enemies, the presence of a large collection of silkworms is sure to attract other enemies; crows, wasps, and the ichneumon by day, bats, owls, and rats by night, will, unless guarded against, destroy great numbers of the silkworms.

" The silkworms themselves are prevented from leaving the tree by bands of some smooth substance, such as fresh plantain leaves, over which they cannot crawl. If all the food of the tree has been eaten they are allowed to descend, and collected and put on another tree. When about to spin they will descend the trunk until arrested by the plantain leaves; they are then collected in baskets, and over these baskets are suspended branches of dried leaves, up which they crawl and form their cocoons. Many silkworms drop off the trees, and the ground under the trees on which they feed should therefore be kept clear, to enable them to be easily found and replaced on the tree. Continual heavy rain is apt to wash them off the tree, but otherwise they seem to be able to protect themselves from rain by crawling under the leaves.

"It remains now only to explain how the cocoons should be dealt with when obtained. The cocoons will be known to be completed by the absence of any sound within. The first care will naturally be to select a sufficient number for breeding purposes. Many of the silkworms die before the completing of the spinning of the cocoon. These are of course no use for the present purpose. They may be distinguished generally by their being smaller, and in an incomplete condition, and by a hollow sound they yield when gently tapped. About an equal number of males and females are usually selected. The females may be generally distinguished by being larger than the males, and of a more symmetrical shape. The males have the cocoons somewhat irregular in shape, as if pinched at one end. These are kept together in suitable places until they burst into the moth. The eggs are generally laid in one or two days, after which the moths die.

"In the case of silkworms which have been classed as wholly domesticated, neither in the stage of the moth, nor in that of the silkworm, is there any tendency to roam. But in the case of the partially domesticated worms, some care has to be taken to provide against this tendency, while at the same time the moths must not be frightened by too severe restrictions.

"A curious fact which has been noted in regard to these partially domesticated moths is that it frequently happens that if a female moth be fastened out at a convenient place at night, a wild male moth will discover and impregnate the former. This fact is sometimes made use of to strengthen the breed of comparatively wild silkworms, which seem often to deteriorate under domestication.

"Of the remaining cocoons, after the selection has been made for breeding a further sorting will have to be made.

"The French growers sort the cocoons of the single common silkworm (Bombyx mori) into as many as nine varieties, distinguishing the good ones from those in which the worm has died, and making other distinctions required by the trade. The reeling of silk from the cocoons is nearly all done on the continent of Europe, and principally in the South of France. As a branch of manufacture, reeling is unknown in England, which latter country only works up the reeled silk. The trade in cocoons would therefore be, at least at first, with France, and for the purpose of ascertaining what assortment of cocoons was required, it would be necessary for the grower to put himself in communication, through his agents or otherwise, with the manufacturers of that country. There would be no difficulty whatever in this, and when once it were ascertained in what manner the cocoons should be sorted, there ought to be little practical difficulty in sorting them. In despatching specimen bales the point of importance would naturally be to make the bales as like the samples as possible; and probably at first it would be well to make as many distinctions in the cocoons as were readily noticeable, and to err on the side of over minute distinctions rather than otherwise. The manufacturers would at once point out which distinctions were of importance, and which not so."

I am glad to state the other diagrams were prepared for me by Mr. Rider, a pupil of the Leek Art Class. The maps showing the wild silk districts were done by Mr. Alfred Moore, of Leek, and I have been much helped in the microscopic work by my assistant, Mr. Rigby, and I must not omit to mention the assistance rendered me by my printing staff.

It is a fallacy, held by some entomologists, that the worm twists the two threads together as it forms them at the orifice of its spinnarets, in all species, both *Bombycidæ* and *Saturniidæ*. The two threads are simply laid side by side, as you see in the diagrams. It would be impossible to twist the two threads without the worm itself revolving continuously with the emission of the silk, or for it to have spinning wheels at the secreting orifice. I propose, therefore, to change the word spinnaret, which conveys an inaccurate impression, and substitute for it seripositor.

Leaving now the more beaten track of the natural history side of the question, I come to speak of its merchantable and art side. Finding, many years ago, that Tusser silk opposed a resistance in no ordinary degree to tinctorial matter, I took an interest in the subject with a view of overcoming this resistance. In its small affinity, ordinarily speaking, for colouring matter, it ranks with the vegetable fibres of cotton and flax, and whilst, in many processes, it would come out scarcely tinted, the mulberry-bred silk would be found to have seized the colour with avidity. It, however, takes the aniline dyes, under certain conditions, moderately well. At that time, and for some years previously, little Tusser silk had passed through the dye-houses. About forty years ago an attempt was made to introduce it in Macclesfield for sewing silk for black, but, on account of its irregular way of taking the dye, it was abandoned. Mr. David Clarke, of Macclesfield, at that time, with his father, Mr. Jeremiah Clarke, were much interested in bringing it to the front; but, as Mr. D. Clarke informs me, the second parcel not coming from the dyer in a saleable state, a costly trial took place at Chester to determine whether the blame lay with the dyer or the silk. I believe it was decided in favour of the manufacturer, and against the dyer, who, unfortunately for him, had succeeded in dyeing the sample parcel successfully. However, the result was that little or no Tusser silk has been used for sewing purposes from that day to this. About twelve years ago I made many experiments in dyeing this silk, and had the satisfaction of seeing my way to further utilisation and improvement. In 1873, the firm of which I am senior partner, consisting of my brother and myself, exhibited, at the International Exhibition at South Kensington, the result of progress up to that time, in a series of black and coloured silks, which were in advance of any similar effort, either English or Continental, as far as my observations or knowledge extended, and they attracted a good deal of attention and led to a further utilisation of Tusser silk, then a drag in the market, except for dress silks for women and girls in the undyed and pleasing shade natural to it, which is fawn colour.'

The development up to that time had been that this silk could be dyed into any middle or dark shade of drab, slate, brown, green, violet, or dark red, whilst, to pale shades of blues, pinks, cerise, scarlet, and others, the dark natural ground colour of the silk interposed an insuperable barrier, as sulphur, or any then known bleaching agent, could not reduce the silk to a whiter state. The *desideratum* of pale shades led our quick French neighbours to study the composition of the brown colouring matter, and to find a solvent for it. The credit of this achievement must be awarded to M. Tessié du Motay, who was led to try permanganate of potash, which was at that time attracting much attention on account of its great oxidising power on organic matter. He found the browny colorant yielded to this agent. Unfortunately, the oxidising action being too violent, the fibre of the silk as well as its coloration was affected, and the silk was tendered by the time it became white enough for dyeing into pale colours so much as to render it useless. However, a secret had been discovered, and it was this: that oxygen, under certain combining conditions, united with the colouring matter, which then became separated from the silk. The object now was to apply the oxygen under gentler conditions. This M. Tessié du Motay again succeeded in doing, and in a very ingenious way. He brought into contact with the silk an insoluble body, which, on contact, should yield up an atom of oxygen in the nascent form, which should gently unite with the fawn-coloured matter of the silk without attacking the fibre. This, although a rough method, solved the difficulty, and the silk, originally of the colour of this sample, can now be bleached in this way to that of the sample I show you, which is of sufficiently pale a ground to admit of its being dyed into any pale colour except white. The substance he found to comply with the required condition is binoxide of barium. Unfortunately, the process is too expensive, and prevents an extensive utilisation of Tusser silk, but there is a probability of the principle being shortly applied by other methods, which will be at the same time cheaper and more within the legitimate sphere of dye-house technical operation than that of M. Tessié du Motay, I mean, whereby the nascent oxygen shall be presented to the silk in the vat from a solution, instead of from a solid, as at present.

Major Coussmaker remarks, that if the worms could be caused to void all their cement (which he supposes to be acid, urate of ammonia, with some phosphate of lime) before spinning, nearly pure white cocoons would be obtained. He has sent me a Tusser cocoon almost as white as the mulberry silk cocoons from China, of which the caterpillar was not allowed to complete its cocoon on the tree, but kept on voiding the cement till it found a quiet nook.

In Germany, I am informed by Mr. Spindler, a large dyer at Berlin, that he is dyeing this silk in considerable quantities for passementerie purposes, for which it is admirably suited. I had manufactured for him samples for his first trials here.

For the production of bright and fast colours on Tusser silk I have found the F process, described in my report on the examination of the dyestuffs of India, to be best adapted, as a general rule, especially in the case of yellow colours.

In 1874 I had the honour to receive a communication from Sir Louis Mallet, Under-Secretary of State for India, asking me to communicate, " for the informa-

"tion of the Government of India, any details I might be in a position to furnish "on the subject of dyeing the wild silk produced by the Tusser worm."

On my report being received, I was requested to make a full investigation of the subject, which divided itself naturally into two heads: a consideration of the silk and of tinctorial matters. For the first, I found the raw silk as it comes into this country to be prepared by the natives of India and China in such a rude and filthy state as to interpose unnecessary obstacles to its taking the dyes. I felt sure that cleaner and more skilful methods of reeling and preparing the silk for the market would be accompanied by less resistance to tinctorial matter, as well as furnishing a greatly improved quality. At my request orders were issued for the collection in the different provinces of India of a complete assortment of native dyestuffs, as well as a supply of Tusser silk.

In recommending the Government of India to have the natives taught the dyeing of their wild silks with dyestuffs indigenous to India I had two motives, one to prevent the native art of India being tampered with by the introduction of European fugitive dyes and crude colours, and another that they could be made to utilise what their country has ever been so rich in—the remarkable variety of native-grown dyestuffs which in other than wild silk fabrics they have known probably for thousands of years so well how to use. To take dyestuffs to India must surely be carrying coals to Newcastle. I have since received an extensive and most interesting series of India dyestuffs and tanning materials, which I have at present under examination. I also received a quantity of Tusser cocoons, and not being able to have them reeled in England, I was authorised to go to Italy to see if I could have them reeled there, and effect my hope for improvement in the manufacture. By the introduction of a friend I obtained permission to visit one of the filatures in Piedmont, that of Messrs. Gaddum and Co. On arriving there I found an extensive mulberry silk reeling and throwing establishment, situated in a most beautiful valley in one of the southern spurs of the Alps, about three hours' journey north of Turin.

On explaining my mission, and showing the wild cocoons, I was told there was not much chance of success, for they had several times tried them, and had found them difficult to soften and impracticable to work; but, knowing too well how natural is the tendency of mankind in any new idea to suggest objections rather than the means, I asked for permission to be allowed to try myself. The permission being generously granted, and every assistance kindly afforded me, I was taken to the reeling room, where about 100 young women were at work, with well-trained fingers, reeling the small Piedmont cocoons of *Bombyx mori*. The operation was interesting in the extreme, heightened as it was by their strange singing of old French songs, in a dialect not even understood by the Italians, a strange and all but forgotten tongue, which has to be learned by the mill-overlookers before they can communicate their instructions to them. I was told these girls were the descendants of Huguenot refugees, escaped probably from Provence to the Italian side of the Alps at the Revocation of the Edict of Nantes, and that they still retained their patois and their folk-lore; they worked hard for the few months of cocoon reeling, from five in the morning until eight at night, for a franc a day; after work dancing and singing for the hour before bedtime in the most joyous way. Apartments are provided for them at the factory, and when the reeling season is over they separate and return to their Alpine villages, to wait for the next season's work.

The operation of unwinding silk from the cocoon is as follows:—A number of cocoons are immersed in an iron pan, in water nearly boiling, with a little alkali to soften them. A semi-rotating brush is placed over them, which quickly catches the exterior fibres of each cocoon, and the more readily enables the reeler to find the windable thread. They are then taken out and transferred to the reeler, who sits leaning over an iron pan of about 12 inches in diameter, in which she has a few cocoons in hot water, the found ends of several being in one hand. Four or six cocoons, as the case may be, are being simultaneously reeled into a single thread by the reel at her back which draws off over her head the cocoon threads, they dancing and turning in the water. When a thread breaks, or the cocoon is reeled, another is quickly presented from the lot in the other hand, the manipulation being one of great dexterity. Several years are required to attain proficiency, and it is not until the fifth to the seventh year that a reeler is entrusted with the most delicate reeling; the keeping of the size of the thread regular and free from rough places being the most important attainment.

It is in this branch of the manufacture that Tusser silk is so defectively treated in India, the reeling being done in some instances round the naked knee cap, but generally with hand reels like this specimen.

I took some of my wild cocoons, and, with much difficulty and patience, after several trials, succeeded in softening them by the aid of long-continued boiling in water, to which was added soap, potash, and glycerine. When soft enough, one of the most skilled girls was told off to reel them for me, and, after ridding the cocoons of the outer and coarser threads, she reeled the threads of four cocoons into one, almost without a break, much to her own delight and to the surprise of my friends and myself.

The next day, the resulting Tusser raw silk was taken to the throwing mill, and there made into Organzine and Tram, of such fineness as to surprise my friends, who said that they had no idea that Tusser silk could be made so fine, and that they should think seriously about sending a person to India to collect Tusser cocoons, that their workpeople might wind them after their mulberry crop had been finished.

The usual size—that is, thickness—of thread of Tusser raw silk of commerce is 152 to 255 deniers—that is, skeins of 1,000 yards long, weighing 9 to 15 drams. From some of the finer raw silk a size of 6 to 7 drams is obtained, but it is generally coarser. From the cocoons, the reeling of which I superintended, I obtained a size of 51 deniers, or three drams per 1,000 yards, a sample of which I have the pleasure to show you.

It is difficult to say how much silk one person can reel per day with the usual method, as it very much varies according to the quality of the cocoons, the sizes, whether you reel current qualities or extra classics, specialities for crêpe, tulle, &c. Perhaps 160 (5$\frac{9}{14}$ oz.) to 360 grams (12$\frac{19}{28}$ oz.) per day would be near the mark.

Here are samples of Tusser raw and thrown silk I have received from M. H. Meyer, of Milan, obtained from cocoons I sent him. The size of the raw is 23–27 deniers, or 1$\frac{1}{2}$ drams per 1,000 yards; the Organzine and Tram are 50–55 deniers, or 3 drams. He found some of my cocoons very difficult to reel, no doubt owing to their age, and to not having been reeled before weather exposure. Fourteen pounds and a half yielded one pound of raw silk. He informs me that some cocoons he has just purchased in Marseilles are larger in size than those I sent him; they are darker in colour, but reel much better. He is obtaining from ten pounds of them one pound of raw silk.

Even a finer thread might be obtained, but as the fibre is only the $\frac{1}{710}$th part of an inch, or three times as thick as ordinary silk, I think 51 deniers is a good and practicable limit when native reelers can have proper appliances, and be taught to be as handy as the reelers of Italy or the south of France. I dare say some of my hearers may remember the improvements which took place in reeling the mulberry silks of Bengal and Brutia, when superior skill and machinery were introduced, a good many years ago. Before that time Bengal silks were held in very low estimation, and were very difficult to work, but after the introduction of better appliances, Bengal silk was shown to be as capable of refinement as any other. Brutia silk now commands, by its superior quality, the highest price in the market; and I have no doubt that, in degree, equal success lies waiting for the Tusser silk industry.

I trust I may point to this manufacturing development and great improvement with pardonable pride, more especially as I am not a manufacturer, and could scarcely expect to find untrodden ground in a domain distinct from, although allied to, my own.

The new reeled silk is much lighter in colour, as you see, than native reeled, and has very much more lustre; in fact, it is the most lustrous in the undyed state of all silks, and possesses greater strength and tension. I found, what I expected to find, that the silk thus reeled dyes much more easily, more shades and lighter ones can be dyed upon it than native reeled; it has no disagreeable smell, and only loses two ounces per pound in being cleaned for dyeing, where native reeled Tusser loses in some cases as much as six to seven ounces per pound, and never less than four to five ounces. It is as clean, to use a technical term, which means free from slubs and irregularities of thread, as ordinary silk. The cost of reeling new and good cocoons, and manufacturing them into Organzine and Tram, is about seven shillings per pound, and it is certain to make its way in many fabrics where extreme fineness is not required, and for a variety of purposes in passementerie, trimmings, braids, scarves, broad and narrow goods. It is beginning to be largely used for these purposes in France. Its price has lately risen, whilst that of other silks has either remained stationary, or actually depreciated.

Mr. Coussmaker remarks, in a letter to me from Poona, that the Bombay mills can spin 2/30 Tusser yarn and weave cloth therefrom at a total charge, including the cost of collecting the cocoons in the jungle, of R. 1 8 a., *i.e.*, 3*s*., per yard of 20″, and that when the work is regularly started it can be done cheaper. He also says that there seems to be a general opinion among the Europeans in his district that the cloth would be readily bought up at the above rate.

I have urged on the Government of India the importance of introducing to the natives of India the European modes of reeling cocoons, and some time ago drew their attention to an invention which simplifies and economises this operation.

Mr. Mackenzie, engineer, of Milan, has introduced a Milan house of filateurs, who have invented and patented another mode of reeling, by which skilled labour is dispensed with. If this machine is pronounced by experts to be a success, there is no reason why cocoon reeling should not be carried on in any village home, as flax spinning was formerly.

M. David, the largest ribbon manufacturer in St. Etienne, seeing this improved manufacture and dyeing in the Indian Section of the Paris Exhibition, where they were first displayed, offered to buy all the cocoons produced in India, if the price would not be more than one franc per kilogramme, a price which Dr. Birdwood assures me is reasonable. He has applied to the India Government for 2,000 kilogrammes of cocoons for experiments at his own cost. It would be a very good thing for a trade to spring up in Tusser cocoons. The natives could easily be encouraged to breed a larger supply, whilst improvements in reeling would require time, and would meet with obstacles of race, religion, and habit difficult to overcome; also the enterprise in this direction would have to be purely private and mercantile, as I think the Government of India would not enter into commercial undertakings, but would probably, and certainly ought to, give most strenuous encouragement and help to stimulate the further spread of this most interesting industry.

I was requested by Dr. Birdwood last year to exhibit the developments of which Tusser silk was capable in the Indian Section of the Paris Exhibition. Sir P. Cunliffe Owen entered most warmly into the idea, and took the greatest interest in it throughout, giving me all the encouragement and help required to make it worthy of being represented side by side with the beautiful objects in which India had determined to assert herself. In no exhibition before had India been shown in a manner so worthy of the gorgeous East. It was the India of the artist which asserted itself at Paris—the old historic land, from which art manufactures in brocades, printed calicoes, jewellery, ivory carving, and pottery may still draw their highest aspirations. Neither had ever before been so much done for the promotion of Indian commerce. These results are entirely due to Sir P. Cunliffe Owen, and to one who so ably assisted him, Mr. C. P. Clarke.

In the wild silk exhibits which I was entrusted to bring together in this Section, not only were the improvements shown in manufacturing and dyeing, to which I have alluded, but another and more decorative phase, and one developed, so far as I can gather, for the first time in the history of either the East or the West—that of printing. It had struck me that fabrics made of Tusser silk, either of native or home manufacture, would be susceptible of much enrichment if they could be printed upon. After many fruitless attempts, I at last succeeded, and since that time I have had the satisfaction of succeeding in applying and fixing a much wider range of colours.

Thinking that designs of an Eastern type were naturally the most applicable to cloths of this wild silk, I have obtained, by the courtesy of Dr. Forbes Watson, the loan of a large series of wood printing blocks, of native design and workmanship, from the India Museum. I have used them for printing nearly all the illustrations of my lecture, and have placed a few on the table, to show how beautifully they are cut. In England the finer details would be in copper, but in these the hardest wood has been chosen and most skilfully cut. To complete the consistency, I have adhered to the use of native Indian colours and colouring matters. You will notice the deep rich red of the India print in madder or munjeet, the good toned and permanent indigo shades, as well as a variety of other well-known native dyes. The designs on these blocks are extremely interesting, and if I had time to exhibit the whole series of the impressions I have taken from them, I am sure you would agree with me how they abound in originality and beautiful drawing. If from this we are led to think generally of the native art of India, we may justly feel some sorrow and regret that our influence there does not tend to perpetuate it, and regret with Dr. Birdwood, as he so well describes in his handbook, that it daily deteriorates. If it were not that Sir Cunliffe Owen is sitting so near to me, I might be led to suggest whether we could not try the experiment of turning the tables somewhat, and that if we must send our art masters to India we might at least import some from there to try to bring us into better ways.

Truly our credentials to teach an artistic people are in a sad condition; if we take but architecture, for example, we are but copyists. Imitation seems to be the evil genius of our time, and even what little originality we have to be thankful for in decorative or structural art is no sooner born than it is preyed upon by an unprincipled selfishness and rascality, which, in the greed for gain in such matters, sees no distinction between *meum* and *tuum*; whilst, on the other hand, so strong is the existing jealousy to protect that which should benefit all, that we may scarcely with safety look over our neighbour's palings to see how green his lawn is.

I would call attention to the sweetness with which the colours repose on the natural and unbleached ground of the cloth, as well as the greater sharpness and depth of those printed on bleached grounds.

Many of my examples are painted in print colours on outline printed designs, an ancient and most interesting mode of decorating cloth, which I have revived.

In addition to the examples I prepared for my lecture, I send others which show further progress, and not the least interesting, the application of gold and silver printing, so called, suitable for both dress and furniture purposes. *See* Nos. 11 and 12.

I think you will agree with me that the material so decorated is beautifully suited to wall hangings, curtains, coverlits, and all kinds of furniture work, and whilst not having quite the brilliancy of the mulberry silk in its printed state, it has a richer and softer surface than those of cretonnes or challis, whilst its lasting qualities are superior to those of any other material.

I am pleased to be able to state that in consequence of the information given to France by the Tusser silk prints exhibited in the India section of the Paris Exhibition, the French took so much interest in the matter as at once to apply the discoveries in printing Tusser silk, and have consequently made Tusser prints fashionable this season both in France and England for ladies' dresses and pompadours.

Messrs. Durant, of London, have kindly informed me that the bulk of Tusser raw silk at present sent into the English market comes from China, and they believe the large shipments of two years ago were principally owing to the famine in the districts of productions. Scarcely a bale, they say, has come forward during the present season, nor do they expect any at the present prices. The present price of Tusser raw silk in London is 4*s*. 6*d*. per lb. The stock in London is China Tussore. It is collected in the district of Chefoo, and shipped from Shanghai. The price of Indian Tussore cloth is about 2*s*. per yard, 34 inches wide.

Tusser silk is now becoming very scarce; the price also, which was in 1877 and 1878 as low as 2*s*. 6*d*. per lb., and large stocks since consumed could not find purchasers, is now 7*s*. to 9*s*. per lb., and the raw much inquired for.

There is a very large quantity of China Tusser cloth exported from London to the Colonies. An immense trade would be developed in India if better qualities were woven there.

Tusser.

The following table shows the state of the London market in Tusser silk for the last few years :—

Year.	Stock, January 1st.	Imported.	Consumed.
	Bales.	Bales.	Bales.
1874	662	None.	168
1875	494	None.	319
1876	175	427	174
1877	428	1,037	284
1878	1,181	837	736
1879	1,282	—	145
1880	194	—	—

The stock, February 1st, was 1,137 bales, with a consumption for January of 145 bales. Should the demand continue at this rate, the supply would be insufficient for the year if no more comes in.

The average consumption for the four years ending 1877 was 238 bales, whilst the consumption for 1878, the year that attention was drawn to it by the Paris exhibits, more than trebled itself, the purchases being 736 bales for that year.

The following table shows present prices of silks in the London market (April 18th, 1879):—

	s.	d.
China raw Tsatlee, No. 4, per lb. - - -	15	6
Canton raw, No. 1, per lb. - - -	13	6
„ „ No. 4, „ - - - -	11	6
Japan raw Marbush, No. 2½, per lb. - -	16	0
Italian Organzine - - - - -	25	0
Bengal raw - - - - - -	14	6
Brutia raw - - - - -	23	0
Tusser raw - - - - - -	4	6

The great improvements made in this country and on the Continent of late years in carding and spinning machinery have enabled manufacturers to utilise all the silk that could not be reeled, such as pierced cocoons and all kinds of waste silk.

Mr. Clayton has been kind enough to lend me for my lecture illustrations of this useful phase of manufacture, specimens of spun Tusser silk in each stage of manufacture, from the first carding or dressing operations to such perfected fabrics as you see before you in cloths of varied design and substance, yarns for weaving and sewing, and shawls in plain and printed states.

There is now a great demand for Tusser and other wild silk waste, and England possesses more than sufficient machinery to spin all that can be imported.

Another form for the use of Tusser silk is the manufacture of embroidery silks, and their application to cloth by the needle. I have had manufactured a few silks which have been arranged by my wife for illustration this evening. She has also worked a few pieces of Tusser cloth in these silks in various designs. The larger piece of embroidery, which is unfinished, is a trial piece. Mrs. Wardle began to work first with untwisted silk, which, as may be observed at the left corner of the work, has a fluffy appearance; therefore, I recommend for embroidery purposes a slightly twisted silk, which I think will be an improvement on crewels, and possibly filoselles, and so prove a useful industry.

Discussion.

A meeting of the Indian Section of the Society of Arts was held on Friday, May 2nd; Sir P. Cunliffe Owen, C.B., K.C.M.G., in the chair, when Mr. Thomas Wardle, F.C.S., F.G.S., read a paper on "The Wild Silks of India, principally Tusser."

The Chairman, in introducing Mr. Wardle, said this evening's subject was one of the most practical results of the Paris Exhibition. There was nothing which more interested the French people than Mr. Wardle's collection, and India was specially honoured by the International Jury in receiving the Grand Medal of Honour for silks as well as for tea. The manufacturers from Lyons were greatly interested in the Indian collection, notwithstanding it was contained in a very unpretending set of cases; and he must confess that when this matter was first brought under his notice by Dr. Birdwood, he did not think anybody could have had an idea of the practical results which would be achieved by Mr. Wardle's efforts. Mr. Wardle had been for some years employed by the India Office in making inquiries as to the development of this industry, and particularly as to the application of dyes from the plants to be found in the neighbourhood in which the silks were obtained. One could always see the mistakes which had been made after a thing was over, and he certainly thought those in charge of the Indian collection (of which he himself was one) might have taken more trouble in developing it. Mr. Wardle had great difficulties to contend with, but notwithstanding, he would repeat that the specimens of silk now exhibited were the most practical results of any International Exhibition, and Englishmen might be proud to think that the Empire of India had come out with such glorious results; but he was afraid many of them hardly realised what Mr. Wardle had done. The Lyons manufacturers, however, saw the importance of it; they were now in correspondence with him, and were anxious that his paper should be read before the Lyons Chamber of Commerce.

Mr. Wardle then read his paper, as printed in the preceding pages, after which there was the following discussion:—

Dr. Birdwood said:—Ptolemy was the first to use the word *Serice* for China, or rather, the northern part of it, known later as Cathay; and the word is derived from the Chinese name of the silkworm, *see*, in Corean *sir*, whence the Greek Σήρ, the silkworm; Σῆρες, the people furnishing silk. The Latin *sericum* had been traced direct to the Mongol *sirkeh;* and the *serikoth* of Isaiah xix. 9 has been supposed to be silk. If the latter identification is correct, the trade in silk between the East and West went back to the remotest antiquity. But there is no undoubted proof of a knowledge of silk in Europe until the time of Alexander. Aristotle certainly describes the silkworm, and the Greeks of Alexander's expedition must have seen both Chinese and Indian silks in India, and Tusser cocoons. When Chinese silks and the manufacture of Tusser silk were first introduced into India is also an obscure question. In the *Ramayana* silks are mentioned among the presents made to Sita, the bride of Rama; but whether these were of Chinese or native manufacture cannot be determined. In the *Mahabharata* it is said that the "Chinas, Hunas, Kashas, and Cauchas, who lived in the mountains," brought as tribute to Yudhestra "silk and silkworms." If the "Chinas" here really were Chinese the question would be settled. But I believe Colonel Yule has somewhere stated that the "Chinas" of the *Mahabharata* were some tribe of the North-western Himalayas, near to the Dards; and so everything is left in obscurity as to the first introduction of Chinese silk into India. It is not even known whether the Arabs, on their first arrival in India, found the silk manufacture already going on there, or introduced it themselves. Pliny's account of the silkworm is taken from Aristotle, but he knew Chinese silk well, and he also tells us that in his time the wild silk of the Tigris valley was woven into gauze. Pausanias, about 100 years later, also describes the silkworm; and the allusions to Chinese silk by the Roman poets from the time of Augustus are too numerous to cite; but it is clear that before the time of Julius Cæsar silk was but little known in Europe. Procopius, about A.D. 550, tells the story of the introduction of the silkworm's eggs into Constantinople in the reign of Justinian, and how the culture of silkworms and the manufacture of silk spread from that time all over Southern Europe is a thrice-told tale. Mr. Wardle has been so good as to refer to my report of 1858 on Tusser. I would wish to state that the first person to suggest the utilisation of Tusser cocoons in Bombay was the late Mr. Edwin Heycock. A meeting was held in Bombay, in 1857, to found the Victoria and Albert Museum, and Mr. Heycock, in pointing out how useful it would be in bringing jungle products into public notice, instanced the waste of Tusser cocoons in the Bombay Presidency, simply through the ignorance of merchants in Bombay of their existence. I reported the matter to Government, and a large quantity of cocoons were at once sent to this country, and inquiries made all over the Presidency, which elicited the fact that Tusser cocoons were as abundant in Bombay as in Bengal. Afterwards Major Coussmaker and Dr. McKenzie paid great attention to the matter, when, at last, the task of practically investigating the comparative commercial value of Tusser silk was fortunately taken up by Mr. Wardle. His paper has scarcely done justice to his own labours in the matter. It is perhaps to encyclopædiac, and at the same time, says too little of his own experiments and their practical results; and as I know more of Mr. Wardle's work than perhaps anyone else in the room, I doubly regret that I am under the necessity of having to leave at once. Briefly, Mr. Wardle, has at last, after years of patient research, succeeded in spinning Tusser silk as fine as the finest Chinese silk, and in giving to it every tincture which Chinese silk will receive. He has thus made it merchantable wherever silk is reeled, spun, woven, dyed, printed, or used for personal or household adornment. Here is the prospect of a great gain for India, and Mr. Wardle deserves for it the grateful acknowledgment of everyone interested in the welfare of India. Sir Philip Cunliffe Owen said he regretted not having put Mr. Wardle's exhibits more forward at Paris last year; but I am an eye-witness to the fact that Sir Philip did everything in his power to promote the deep interest of India in Mr. Wardle's work. Universal attention was drawn to it in Paris, and if, henceforth, Tusser becomes a yearly growing article of export from India, the result will be almost as much due to

Sir Philip Cunliffe Owen as to Mr. Wardle. I must add that I was perfectly astonished on entering the room and seeing the samples of printed Tusser—in Indian dyes, and stamped with Indian blocks — exhibited here to-night by Mr. Wardle. I could not have believed it possible for him to have made such progress in the short time since I saw his last tentative efforts; but while I congratulate him on the taste and ability in the dyer's art these beautiful fabrics show him to possess, I cannot altogether wish him success in his imitation of Indian designs. Imitation is no more good for us than the natives of India, nor is it possible to welcome these efforts to take a manufacture out of their hands simply because, being rulers in India, we are in a position to force their hands.

Mr. Francis Cobb said there was no doubt that the demand for this silk had increased recently, partly in consequence of a change in fashion. There had been a run on it by the French; and, owing to the change in the method of dyeing, almost every colour, even of pale rose, could now be dyed. How much was worked up in the fabrics which were supposed to be all genuine China silks he believed it was impossible to say, especially those subject to heavy dyes. During the last two years the demand in China for this Tusser silk for France had been so great as to seriously interfere with the supply required for the country, which, as it was the cheap silk of the country, was very large. The French had now pretty well exhausted China, and hence one great cause of the anxiety which was noticed at the Exhibition; they were all aware that they were fast exhausting China, and turned with the greatest delight to the specimens received from India, showing that there was a new field open to them. He trusted, however, that the whole of the industry was not destined to find its way to France. Although they had made some rapid strides there, we had also been leading the way in this country, and but for the fact that they beat us in the cost of labour, he had no doubt that the Tusser industry would have developed itself to a greater extent here than in France. He might say that the *Atticus ricini* was a worm which was a good colonist—it might be taken to almost any of the colonies and it would thrive. It fed on the castor-oil plant, which grew wild in most of our colonies. For instance, in South Africa, when land was cleared a castor-oil plant would immediately spring up. Mr. Wardle had shown how valuable that particular silk was, and it might be grown to a very large extent in the colonies. He did not believe that these Tusser silks, now that attention had been called to them, would ever go out of demand, and all that India or our colonies could send would find a ready sale for many years to come. The ailanthus, of which they had heard so much seven or eight years ago, and to which Lady Dorothy Neville devoted a great deal of attention, seemed to have failed, and the reason was that the labour expended upon it did not produce a result which would pay its cost. He doubted whether in such a country as this we could ever rear the ailanthus worm to a profit. When he was giving a great deal of attention to this matter some time ago he remembered being informed that there were thousands and thousands of acres of trees in Assam which were infested, as it was termed, with these wild silkworms, and that they only required gathering. He presumed that was the Moonga which Mr. Wardle had spoken of. In the north of Ceylon again there was a large forest district of which very little was known, but there was a cocoon found which was open at the end, and the silk came up there and formed a loop. When that cocoon was treated with caustic soda, or potash, it became softened, so that it could be reeled pretty readily, but he had grave doubts whether reeling was ever worth the trouble and cost for any of these Tussers. Although Mr. Wardle had succeeded in producing very fine reeled silk in Italy, when that silk was completed and reeled it was not equal to China or Italian silk in the same condition, and he doubted whether it was a kind from which we should ever get any very fine results. He would rather adopt Dr. Birdwood's suggestion, and take the coarser manufactures of this silk, and trust to the play of light and shade to produce that rich appearance which he spoke of.

Mr. Wardle said the Tusser silk which came from China appeared to be better reeled, but the reason was that the Chinese reeled the cocoons at once; they did not wait until the chrysalis was killed by heat, and at that time it was more flexible, and had greater elasticity and brilliancy. This was a thing to be noted, and to be introduced into India, to secure the cocoons whilst the chrysalis was still in them, and thus to produce them in a condition in which the silk might be spun. No doubt M. David would be very glad to get a great deal of this silk for one franc per kilogramme, which Dr. Birdwood thought a reasonable offer; but he thought there would be no difficulty in selling it in this country for two shillings per kilogramme. He did not think that it was the price which stopped the supply, but, rather, that it was the French demand, which had pretty well cleared all the available silk from China, and that they would not send any more, except at a very enhanced price. With regard to the difficulty in dyeing, he believed that had been overcome by Mr. Wardle. He had been as yet unable to find out how it was done in France, and the last answer he got to his pertinacity was, that he was not likely to find out, as it was a trade secret. Still, he had hopes that Mr. Wardle, in his persevering manner, would eventually find this out for himself, and would be able to compete with the French, even in the most delicate light colours. The exhibit he had shown was the most remarkable he had ever seen, and the dyes were such as, a few years ago, he should have thought were impossible.

Mr. Davenport said Mr. Clayton, who had exhibited some of this Tusser silk at the Paris Exhibition, was present, and he hoped he would give them some information upon it.

Mr. Wardle said he wished to supply an accidental omission in his lecture, and that was with regard to the adaptability of Tusser silk for spinning. He had there some beautiful manufactures of spun Tusser silk, but unfortunately they had been so delayed by the railway, that they only arrived at the last moment after his lecture had gone to press. They had been kindly lent by Messrs. Clayton; Mr. Clayton was present, and he hoped would explain them.

Mr. Clayton said that some four or five years ago a large shipment of Tusser waste came over here, and was lying about a long time in Lower Thames Street. From thence it was taken to Manchester, where it also lay for two or three years, as no one would look at it. He accidentally came across some samples, and determined to try some experiments. The first trial was so promising that he got further samples, and the result was that they showed some of the sliver to the firm of Sir Titus Salt and Co., with the idea that this silk could be mixed with brown mohair, which that firm were spinning at that time. They at once asked him not to mention it to anyone else, but to get a few skeins of sliver prepared, and to bespeak the whole parcel of this material. They got an order for 1,000 weight, but in working it up Messrs. Salt discovered some hitch or defect in the spinning, and had to discontinue it for the purpose originally suggested. His firm had by this time the whole parcel on their hands, and therefore they had to endeavour to utilise it themselves. After repeated experiments they discovered the means of giving it spinning qualities, and they introduced it into the market in the shape of threads for various purposes. The trade had gradually grown, and twelve months ago they had got through the whole parcel of raw Tusser waste, which they found afterwards was all that was brought from China. After those threads and cloths were shown in the market and sold, they found the raw material came over very slowly, and at present there did not seem any prospect of further supplies. This led him to investigate the question of developing the trade from India. They had no longer any of this raw material coming from China. There was not a bale in London, and, as far as he could learn, not one on the way. The importance of this branch of Tusser industry would be apparent when it was remembered, as was stated, that, in the reeling off the cocoon, to obtain one pound of raw silk, ten pounds of waste were made. According to Mr. Wardle's statement, the larger portion of the Tusser cloths came from India, and he was rather at a loss to know what became of the enormous quantity of waste produced in making them, inasmuch as, to his knowledge, none had ever come to this country, except a few pounds. It was, therefore, of great importance to those interested in Indian produce to get at the reason why this waste was not collected and brought to this country. Unless some was brought from India, or elsewhere, the industry would die out for want of raw material.

Mr. A. Rogers said he had seen this very waste being spun in Messrs. Allen's mill, in Bombay. The cocoons were brought in large bales from the jungle just squeezed together, and flattened like a cotton bale. This waste they crushed, and teased it out into very nearly as fine sliver as was shown on the table; and he was perfectly astonished at the cloth made from this waste. He brought home some specimens, and gave them to the Manchester Chamber of Commerce, where, no doubt, they could be seen. Another curious fact which came under his notice was this. There was a man in Bombay, a barber, who made a most remarkable discovery with regard to Tusser silk. He showed him the produce of silk which had been spun by a hybrid worm, produced between the common Indian Tusser worm and what he said was the Japanese Yama-mai. Whether that was the case, he could not say, but he certainly showed him the two worms, which were about the size of his little finger, and he informed him that the silk produced was much freer from tannin than the indigenous Tusser found in the jungle. He showed him some specimens, and so far as he could judge the hybrid silk was far superior to the other. Mr. Morris assured him that this hybrid would feed on the commonest trees in the country, particularly all trees of the fig tribe. If that were the case, and a superior kind of silk could be produced by hybridisation, one could see what an immense future would be open for production, and it would especially afford a means of employment for the mass of the people, especially women. In the higher classes the women were never allowed out of doors, and it would be an inestimable boon if they could be induced to amuse themselves by rearing worms and producing silk. Even in the years of famine, the trees on which the worms fed never failed, so that in such seasons of disaster the existence of this industry would be an immense benefit to the people.

Mr. R. F. Mackenzie, being called upon to describe his machine for reeling silk, which is now at the India Museum, said he had great confidence that it would work Tusser silk admirably. They tried a small experiment with some cocoons, and it had failed, but the failure was not due to any fault in the machinery, or in the softening process, but he discovered from Mr. Moore that the cocoons were 12 years old; consequently, the chrysalides inside had got decomposed, the air and water got inside the cocoons, and they would not float. Of course, if the cocoon was fresh it would not imbibe the water, and he had no doubt the silk could be reeled very finely, because one cocoon of Tusser would yield a thread which could be worked, and two or three threads would be equal to ten of ordinary Bengal silk. His machine was certainly more applicable to a Bengal silk cocoon than to any other, and the chief purpose in inventing it was to work these cocoons in large numbers. Of course it would work every other kind, but the advantage would not be so great. When there were ten cocoons going into one thread, as hand labour was depended upon to feed all those ten threads, it became a serious matter, because it took five or six years to become an expert reeler. In India he did not think they were more expert or intelligent. The machine could be seen at work, on Mondays, Tuesdays, or Wednesdays, at the India Museum, on Indian silk. Hitherto, it had been applied to Italian silk, and had worked admirably. He must say that he was much indebted to the authorities at the India Museum, and to the Indian Government, for the assistance they had given him; and he thought they were all much indebted to the Government for attending to these matters, which, he thought, were quite as important as sending armies to conquer a country. To show how easily it could be worked, he might say that he asked Dr. Forbes Watson if he could procure an intelligent boy or girl to work it, and they were fortunate in getting an intelligent girl of 14. They gave her three hours' instruction, and then set her down to reel. She began with one thread and reeled two threads, which was sometimes equal to twenty cocoons. They were doing Italian cocoons, which were much more easily reeled, and about a week ago she reeled three threads with six cocoons each, and two threads of the Bengal cocoon with ten cocoons each, and he could safely say that the produce would compare with anything ever shown in the London market. They were now making arrangements to send out a staff to India and China to do the thing on an extensive scale. He believed that the Tusser cocoon could be reeled as fine as anything, and it required but few threads. It was true that the threads were flat, and that was a point which made it a little difficult. The only way he could account for that, if he might venture to do so, was from the fact that there was a great amount of woody matter in the Tusser cocoon, and very much less gluten, while there was a great deal of moisture, and no doubt the silk moth used the threads in a very wet state, and in consequence of the great heat it became very hard, and that must flatten the thread to a very great extent. Some time ago there was an idea of introducing cocoons and spinning and reeling them in this country, but it had not been carried out. In Asia Minor, however, and all over France and Italy, it was carried on largely, and he did not see why they should not be reared in England, or why the Indians should not be put in a position to reel from them and to send the organzine and tram to the English market.

Mr. A. Rogers said the introduction of this machine into India would depend a great deal upon the price at which they could be supplied, and a great deal would depend also upon whether the chrysalides required to be killed for the purpose of reeling. A great many of the natives, particularly the followers of Vishnu, were averse to the taking of life in any shape whatever, and though they would spin or do anything with the cocoons gathered in the jungle from which the moths had emerged, they would not do anything with cocoons in which there was a live chrysalis.

Mr. Wardle, in reply, said some of the observations made would be found replied to in parts of the paper which he had not read. Dr. Birdwood did not intend to speak technically when he said that Tusser silk could be made as fine as China, because he did not think that could quite be done. With regard to the danger he feared, of doing injustice to the native people, he could assure them that he shared his feeling; but if the increased cultivation and improvement of this undeveloped industry were worth anything, they must tend to give the natives of India more interest in their work, employ a much larger number, and result in the production of a vastly increased quantity of loudly called-for silk, as the discussion that evening had so satisfactorily shown. He also shared Dr. Birdwood's desire for originality in decoration, but the inventive faculty was an uncommon gift; and there could be no imitation in using for a portion of his lecture-illustrations the actual printing blocks the natives had themselves made and used; it was using the actual ornament, and not a simulation of it. With regard to the suggestion of first dyeing this silk one colour and then another, and thus making two vivid aniline dyes produce a better tone, they had a much quicker and more satisfactory mode of doing it, by simply putting two or more aniline dyes in the vat together. There was no doubt that any artistic colour could be matched with aniline dyes; the only difficulty was that mordants had not yet been discovered for that tinctorial matter, so as to allow the silk to be dyed in permanent colours. Hitherto, they were all more or less fugitive. With regard to Mr. Cobb's interesting speech, he could allay his anxiety with regard to Tusser silk being dyed in weighted blacks in France, and then used to adulterate the best silks. The Tusser worms seemed to share his aversion to heavy blacks, and secreted their silken fibres in such a way that they resisted the weighting processes more than they resisted tinctorial matter. He had known it only increase a few ounces to the pound in an attempt to dye it a heavy black, when China silk had increased 32 ozs.; but with regard to its being mixed with better silk for various articles in colours, it was so used in France last year, and in England at present. With regard to fashion having brought in these silks, he thought it was just the other way, and that it was the fact of Tusser having been made amenable, by improved dyeing, to general requirements, which had led to manufacturers using it. He did not think the French were one whit in advance of what could be done in England in dyeing this silk, both by his own firm and several other principal dyers. The secret which Mr. Cobb could not discover from the French was this, and this only—for he was quite *au courant* with the development of French dyeing (but the air of mystery imparts a charm)—it was the *bleaching* of the silk before dyeing, for unless this were done the pale colours could not be dyed; this effected, the rest was easy. He could have brought all shades of colour, even much paler than what he had shown. He was very glad to hear Mr. Cobb say Tusser cocoons were worth more than M. David estimated them at; so much the better for India. With regard to the late supply of Tusser waste, he was afraid distress in China had something to do with it; but with regard to the waste in India, he did not think there was so much as 12 lbs. to one of silk. The Indians were very economical themselves; in one part of India they used the outer part of the cocoon for making armlets, and even brooches of; but still, if the people could be stimulated to grow more and export it, there would be plenty. With regard to the hybrid worm mentioned by Mr. Rogers, he doubted if he were correct, because the Yama-mai was a Japanese species, which was an oak feeder, whereas the Tusser worm fed on very dissimilar food. Still, it was very probable there had been a hybrid formed between the Tusser and some other kinds. The Tusser cocoon contains no tannin or woody matter. Mr. Wardle concluded by exhibiting a cocoon from South Africa of an immense size, being upwards of a foot long, the inside of which was filled with a number of smaller cocoons, which, he said, was the most curious thing he had ever seen. Still, there was something analogous to be found in some parts of England, minus the matted outer covering.

The Chairman proposed a vote of thanks to Mr. Wardle, not only for the work he had done, but for the modest way in which he spoke of his labours. He knew nothing about the subject himself, but he had taken a great interest in it from the few words he had with Mr. Wardle, about eighteen months ago, when he pointed out the advantages which would accrue from the encouragement of this industry. He would take the opportunity of laying this paper before Sir Louis Mallet and before the Colonial Office, and he hoped some solid advantages would result from the evening's discussion.

The vote of thanks was unanimously passed to Mr. Wardle, and the meeting adjourned.

The Indian silks, diagrams, entomological specimens, &c., shown by Mr. Wardle to illustrate his paper, were borrowed by Messrs. Liberty and Co., of Regent Street, who devoted a special room for their exhibition.